Dancing Feet
in A Man's World

A Woman's Journey
Across Cultures To Herself

Library of Congress Control Number:
ISBN (e-book): 979-8-9890089-1-9
ISBN (paperback): 979-8-9890089-0-2

"Male and Female created He Them." [1]

Dedication

I dedicate this book to my mother
Krishna and my father Din Diyal Khanna
Who brought me into this world
And gave me the inspiration and
The Freedom to soar like an Eagle.

A personal message to the younger generation in my family -
Grandnieces Karishma, Shradha, Suhana, Jasmine, Jiana
(And other younger generation of women)

You can do anything -
Achieve anything that you want
As a woman.
Do not let a man tell you
What you can't do.
Do not let a man interrupt
Your personal and professional dreams.
Do not let anyone degrade you,
For you are strong and
You have the power within you-
You are the Goddesses Durga and Kali-
Who destroyed the demons, whom
No demigods and male Gods could slay-
And you are Goddess Saraswati,
Who holds all wisdom, knowledge, and art,
And you are Goddess Lakshmi
Who all men (and women) worship for
Prosperity and success
And
Above all you are Mother Gaia
Personification of Nature that focuses on
Life-giving and Nurturing aspects of Nature
By embodying it.

Sumedha Mona Khanna

Sumedha Mona Khanna

 Sumedha Khanna, MD, is an obstetrics/ gynecology and public health physician, specialized in women's health programs, national family planning policies and programs, safe motherhood strategies, leadership training for public health, community health, women's health and well-being, and in advocating and teaching integrated well-being practices.

Sumedha (Mona) worked for more than 25 years with the World Health Organization, consulting on Maternal and Child Health, and Public Health in over 60 countries of the world, including the Caribbean, Latin America, Southeast Asia, and Africa. She was the first woman appointed as head of a country office of the WHO and as the director of the Global Health-for-All Strategy and Leadership Development Initiative.

Since her early retirement from WHO (1993), she moved to California with her husband. During 1993-2000, she served as a consultant to several non-profit and health- related agencies in California, including the Public Health Institute, Pacific Institute of Women's Health, and California Women's Health Leadership Program. In 1998, she founded the Healing Well in Gualala, a consulting and information center dedicated to healing and wellness of women in midlife and beyond, with emphasis on healing options and integrating body/mind/spirit practices in daily life.

In 2015, she established the Saraswati Foundation to support higher education and classical dance for girls from low-income families, housing and skills–development for abandoned widows in India, and small relevant community projects in USA.

Sumedha is currently leading an older women's group (age 60 and beyond), exploring lifestyles and choices that support us to remain vital and purposeful till the end of our lives.

This is a personal story of my life's journey, presented in images, stories, and anecdotes, especially to share with the younger generation of girls in my extended family, my nieces and especially my grandnieces. I want them to know about me after I am gone and to be inspired that a woman can do whatever she wants in life. It requires courage, determination, and stamina.

Sumedha Mona Khanna

SHE

She is always there
Within me.
I have sensed her presence
Almost since I was a little girl.
Sometimes, she descends from the blue sky,
Gliding gently, dancing
On a ray of blue light.
Her sensuous, curvy body
Draped in the finest of silks,
Light blue, purple, orange,
Flowing around her body.
Dark long hair to her knees
With flowers, jasmine, gardenia and rose,
She dances down the path of light,
A sensuous smile on her lips.
She, the Apsara of the heavens
Who captivates even the gods,
Yes, She is my companion
My muse, my spirit from
A long time ago.
She resides in me,
Awakens me when I am
Closing in on myself.
Forever restless, yet knowing
What she wants,
She keeps nudging me forward,
Bringing awareness to my life.
Giving birth to new ideas
And rekindles
The fire in my soul.
Makes me want to put on
My dancing bells

And dance to the new tune
My heart wants to sing.
For all that I am
Is truly an expression of
SHE
Who resides in me.

The Psychic

The psychic greeted me at the door of her one-bedroom apartment in her flowing purple robe and long curly graying hair. She took my hand and invited me in. A candle was lit at the altar. The fragrance of incense, lavender and rose, was pervading the entire room adorned with large stuffed pillows on the floor, an Altar in the middle, and other mystical objects all around. The room was dark and mystical. I had to make an effort to focus my eyes. She led me to one of the pillows and bade me to sit. Positioning herself on one of the pillows next to mine, she closed her eyes, invited me to close mine too, and gently held my hand.

After a few minutes of total silence, I became aware of my heartbeat. I noticed a flicker in her closed eyes. My hands became warm and I felt energy flowing into them from her hand. We had "connected".

"I see a beautiful woman. She appears to be from the east. She is wearing a white outfit, long skirt, a blouse, and a long flowing scarf, adorned with silver and gold threads. She is a dancer. She has dancing bells on her henna-painted feet. And I see a young man at the entrance to this hall where this woman is dancing. He is wearing a white and gold outfit. He looks at the woman and turns away and leaves. The woman's feet stop for a second, just a little hesitation. You are this woman. And you have already met this man in this life. He is right now in your life."

I had never been to a psychic before. This woman had never met me. I found out about her from a colleague just a couple of days before I went to see her. Another client had canceled her appointment, so I was able to see her more quickly.

I had met this man recently and my first impulse at our meeting was to dance for him. But that is another story to be told later.

The psychic had seen through my soul. I have no idea how the psychic worked. How did she figure out our past or present lives and dilemmas? But I do know that this woman who had never met me before was able to read my soul.

Dancing Feet in A Man's World

Foreword

This is the story of my life that I have been envisioning in my thoughts – no - in my Spirit, sometimes expressing my thoughts in my journals over the years. I may call it a Spiritual Memoir of my life's journey, maybe also exploring some connections with my past lives. I believe our life is a continuum from before. There is no beginning and no ending. We bring something, anything, that is unresolved from the past into the present life and hope that we can resolve at least some, if not all, that matters. And we may take some other unresolved issues into the next life and so the continuum of life goes on, until we reach a point when all is resolved. We are in search of our true selves... the One that is our pure essence, that has no beginning and no end. It is what it is... the Essence of the Divine. This Final Connection is then made with the Spirit, the Cosmic Consciousness... *All is One here. Nothing is unresolved.*

So, what did I come to resolve this time?

Dancing Feet is the image that comes to mind immediately. This was also revived by the only psychic I have ever met.

I was born with *Dancing Feet*. They were attuned to a rhythm of their own. I could really dance. I never attended a dance class or a dance school. I had no teacher. But my feet moved to any rhythm, any music, any drum automatically. *They knew from before.*

I remember dancing in Moghul courts, dancing for men of status, to please them, to be part of their leisure. I was beautiful. I was admired. Princes, Nawabs, and their sons would come to watch me dance. They would bestow money, jewels, and gifts on me. Many were crazy about me, professed their love to me, but I was detached from their lives. I did not belong to anyone. I was in fact quite aware of their selfish superficiality. They only wanted to have me as their possession. They did not know the meaning of love.

As a helpless dancer, I had no power to control my destiny. Others owned me. They controlled my life. I was only a commodity in their hands, the one that would bring money and prestige for them. In return I would have shelter, food, good clothes, and jewelry to wear - not to own. I had no right to love or move about as I wanted to. I was a just a puppet in men's hands.

The only thing free were my *Dancing Feet*. I danced like no one else could. My soul was in my feet. I danced to the rhythm of my spirit. In time, I *resolved* that I would never again be beholden to men. Deep inside I developed a dislike for that gender. Men were superficial, selfish, power-hungry, and self-centered. They only cared about women because they needed them to take care of their own personal needs. Women were like their slaves, properties, and were beholden to them, because they considered them as their providers.

I probably went through many lives to reach my present one, that placed me in a position to resolve this issue.

I feel that I was born an old soul, very aware of my destiny. In this life, I have crossed many cultures, many boundaries, and have broken many traditions, as well as *Glass Ceilings*. I felt that I was in charge of my life from the beginning. I was fiercely independent. Even as a child I was aware that I would not allow any man to control me or my life. Of this, I was certain. Considering that I was born a third daughter in India, a culture that welcomes sons not daughters, this awareness of the inner power of my spirit was unique.

In this life, I had to be born a girl, a daughter in a culture that traditionally prefers sons over daughters. This was another challenge that I had to confront and conquer. I had to work my way out of traditional pathways that life offers to girls in this culture. I had to become fully independent, both culturally and financially. From a very young age of 3, I knew and insisted that I wanted to become a medical doctor. In India, once a girl qualifies as a medical doctor, her gender does not matter anymore. She earns respect from men and women as a physician. She is no longer addressed as a Miss or Mrs. – she is now a doctor - a gender neutral word. I knew that as a medical doctor I would be financially independent and a respected person. No one argues with a doctor, not even your parents. And I was fortunate enough to have parents who believed in education and independence of women. But I was still in a traditional culture where generally men are in-charge and control women's lives; a culture that expects a young woman to get married at an appropriate age. Even in my case, my mother tried to find a young male doctor for me to marry.

At age 21, I graduated from the medical school in New Delhi, India. This was an all-women medical college, the first and the only one in the world. All students and staff were women and even in the original Will of the Benefactress of the College, it was stated that," No man shall enter these premises." This was later modified to include male faculty but only in the expanded non-clinical departments. So, not only did I qualify as a medical doctor, but I was also taught and influenced by powerful and strong women teachers, many of whom never married. During the entire period of my education, I did not have to deal with or work with men. I became a strong woman with a lot of self-confidence and self-respect.

From an early age I developed a demeanor that I would be better than any man and I worked hard to achieve that. I was totally focused on my career and developing complete independence, professionally and financially, as well as emotionally. I always felt that I had no time to waste, especially on men. With the exception of my father, I did not have respect for men and did not want any to get in my way. So, when marriage proposals began to arrive, I completely rejected them and took off to England at age 23, with the blessings and support of my parents, for higher studies, to become a full-fledged specialist in women's health.

I left India, the land of the Ganges, Yogis, and temples, where Gods and Goddesses are worshiped daily. I spent five formative years in England, while gaining professional expertise. I was also stripping my real identity. My *Dancing Feet* became still. I focused completely on preparing for my professional career that would make me a respected and financially independent woman. After achieving a specialization in Obstetrics and Gynecology, I moved to North America, which opened doors to new opportunities for professional advancement.

Destiny brought me to the predominantly male-dominated international development arena, The United Nations, specifically the World Health Organization. I traveled and worked in many lands, traversed many continents, crossed cultural boundaries, and shattered Glass Ceilings by advancing to senior hierarchical positions that no woman had reached before me.

Much of my professional life was spent in a Man's World. Those were early years in the International Field, with The United Nations and its many specialized agencies. There were very few women at the professional level. Women who worked in the United Nations and its agencies were mostly secretaries, accountants, and in lower echelons of administration. I was an abnormality. Even women in these organizations felt that. Many couldn't get used to the fact that their boss was a woman and were even surprised to see me in the same bathroom facilities that they used. In the Ladies' Room, they spoke in hushed voices or not at all, sometimes even leaving the facility out of surprise.

In this Man's World, as a woman, I learnt a different kind of dance, trying not to become like a man, but learning how to play the game, learning the rules of the game played mostly by men in power, and how to get past them. Games that our mothers never taught us. That was some dance for more than 30 years of my professional life. Even so, I was lucky enough to find a wonderful and mature man who understood me and always facilitated me in my life. He became my life-partner, and we spent 27 years of wonderful life together. I married late (at age 47 years), by which time I felt that I had professionally advanced as much as I wanted to. I feel that had I met him earlier in my life, I might not have been that interested, as I didn't want any man to get in the way of my advancing in my professional career, as well as being financially independent. Even after my marriage, I maintained my financial freedom.

Now, at this winding down phase of my life and once again spending it alone (as my life-partner has passed on), I am reconnecting with my own identity, my Spirit, and of course my *Dancing Feet*. I feel that I have brought closure to the main issues that I brought into this life from my previous life. Now my soul is free to move on to the next phase and life-where there will be no more dancing in a Man's World.

In this life's journey, I have met many fellow-travelers, soul-friends, both men and women (mostly women). I have learnt from them. I have been inspired and supported by them. I believe that one never travels alone. Your life becomes intertwined with many others. You find and recognize many soul-friends. I certainly did.

This is a distilled story of my life's journey in a Man's World, presented in stories, images, and anecdotes. I do believe that it has been a unique journey. I believe that sharing this story with other women, especially younger ones, would validate their journeys and experiences. Even though the world is changing, and women now are in a different place in many societies than they were 50 years ago, this change has not been universal or even enough for women to feel as equal players in life. In many parts of the world, not much has changed for women. In fact, in some places women's status has even worsened. I hope that my story will offer a glimpse of hope and courage to others wanting to break through traditional values, which are still imposed upon women (more than on men). And when these women reach a critical mass, a shift will occur in the consciousness of humanity at large. It will no longer be, a Man's World. Rather, it will be 'One World' with equal rights and opportunities for all.

Table of Contents

1

The Beginning

The Beginning

This is a collage/story of glimpses of my life's journey as a woman, from the ancient Hindu civilization (India is now called a Third World country), to the western world; traversing many countries and regions (more than 60 countries) across cultures, civilizations, and economic and social development statuses.

Many people who meet me for the first time ask me: "Where are you from?".

My answer:

"I was born in India, I grew up in England, and I matured in the Caribbean. Later, I must have acquired some characteristics from Latin America, Africa, Asia, and North America".

So, I feel that I am a citizen of the world, and yes, still grounded in the values that I acquired from my Mother Country, India, land of the ancient civilization, culture, and Vedic wisdom.

My journey in this life began in Delhi, India in a small hospital in Old Delhi, the Victoria Zanana Hospital (women's hospital endowed by Queen Victoria). Even though I was born a third daughter to my parents Din Diyal and Krishna Kumari Khanna, who had expected a second son, I was yet given a powerful message from my mother: "She will be better than a thousand

1

sons!". I inherited this powerful blessing from her arms that held me to her breast at birth.

Born in the Land of the Divine Feminine

Goddesses Yes! Daughters No!

I was born in Delhi, India. India is a land primarily of Hindu Religion, a religion that not only recognizes the power of the Goddesses and of the Divine Feminine, but also worships them. Their images adorn the temples and homes. There are special days in the year devoted specially to the worship of the Goddesses. Twice in a year there are nine-days festivals during which the Goddesses are worshiped. All the major Gods are accompanied by Goddesses and are worshiped together e.g., Vishnu and Lakshmi; Shiva and Parvati; Brahma and Saraswati; Ram and Sita; Krishna and Radha. There are special festivals dedicated to the worship of Goddesses. There are special days when married women fast all day for the long and healthy lives of their husbands. There are no special days when the husbands are expected to do the same for their wives.

There are often contradicting perceptions in Hindu culture concerning women. On one hand, they are expected to be loving, nurturing, submissive, and sensuous. Another image is of the Warrior Goddess, who fights against the demons of injustice. Men who prostrate in the temples in front of the images of Goddesses, can be abusive and treat their women and even their daughters poorly. Most couples and especially the elders in their family want their first born to be a son, who they believe will take care of them when they are older and be there at their cremation to light the funeral pyre. (In the past girls and women were not expected to go to the cremation ceremony and were not allowed to light the funeral pyre. This has been changed legally, but the cultural traditions take much longer to change). Sometimes, the couple will keep trying to have babies until a son is born.

Throughout India's history, there have been remarkable, warrior women. During the early 20th century, India was trying to gain independence from the Colonial British through the Gandhian Movement of Freedom Struggle. This freedom movement led to the liberation of more women who actively participated. Several of my schoolteachers were strong, independent women. Some never married.

What did my being a daughter, a female child, mean?

I grew up in a home where Goddesses were worshiped daily. The statues of Goddesses Durga, Lakshmi, and Saraswati adorned the walls of our home. My mother, a Vedic scholar, was an ardent Goddess worshiper. One of the rooms in our home was kept as a temple, where statues of Gods and Goddesses resided. Every morning and evening my mother would light the Diya (lamp) and worship the Goddesses. This would be after her morning bath and before taking any liquid or food. She observed all Hindu rituals and traditions associated with Goddess worship, including the nine days of Goddess Durga worship that is observed twice a year, around early Spring and late Autumn. This consists of fasting daily for nine days. On the ninth day, special food is prepared at homes and nine girls (before puberty) are invited to the home. They are offered food and gifts. These girls are symbolic of Goddesses. An alternative is for the woman of the home to go to the Goddess temple and offer food and gifts to the priest. (Even in the land where Goddesses are worshiped both by women and men, there are no women priests.)

My mother passed on essential knowledge about Goddesses and their worship rituals to us from childhood. She included her three daughters in the rituals she observed. Sons were not included. But she never enforced any of the rituals on us. Throughout my life, no matter where I have lived, I also have kept a sacred place for worship. Here, the statues and images of Goddesses are always present. I have also chanted special Mantras of Goddesses Durga, Lakshmi, and Saraswati, every day.

The power and blessings of the Divine Feminine have been with me throughout my life. During my school and college study days, Goddess Saraswati dominated my prayers. She is the Goddess of wisdom, education, and the arts. During my main professional period (age 25-55), daily worship of Goddess Durga and Goddess Lakshmi were more prominent, for strength, power, and success. In my later years, Goddess Saraswati has again become dominant in my prayers. I have even named my foundation the Saraswati Foundation and dedicated it to the empowerment of girls and women, through education and literacy.

I was also born during the last decade of the British colonial rule in India. During this period and especially after the Second World War, the Indian Independence movement gained ground. In 1947, eight years after I was born, India won independence. The role of women was strong during these years, many of my schoolteachers were called 'Gandhian Women'. Many of them stayed single and independent. My image of a woman that I formed even during my early years was independent, strong character, educated, could stand on her woman, did not have to marry, fierce yet compassionate, confident, and was even stronger than a man.

My mother had a great influence regarding our belief in the strength and power of the Divine Feminine. I grew up with this belief and my prayers to the Goddesses over my entire life have empowered me to work and progress successfully in what I call "A Man's World".

In the Hindu religion, the combined image of Shiva and Parvati is presented as Ardhangini (half male/half female), incorporating man and woman in one image. This image symbolizes that together the male and female constitute one entity, a unity of

Shiva and Shakti, Yin and Yang. This is a beautiful concept of unity and equality. Even though it remains only a beautiful aspiration, it has been my belief throughout my life and the image of Ardhangini: Shiva and Shakti, adorns my home temple and inspires me every day.

I owe a great deal of my gratitude to my mother who from my childhood instilled in me the belief in the power of the Divine Feminine. I strongly believe that this has given me the strength and power to achieve what I have in a Man's World.

Ardhangini: Half Male and Half Female.

Why I was given the nickname - Mona

At birth I was given a nickname, Munni, which means a little girl for whom no name had been chosen (my parents were expecting a son). My birth, as customary in those days, was simply registered as daughter of Din Diyal Khanna. Later my nickname was changed to Mona when a neighbor's son, who had just returned from the World War, remarked that my smile was like the Mona Lisa. However, according to my birth astrology chart, my name had to start with an initial S. This is why my parents gave me the name **Sumedha,** the name of the daughter of one of my mother's good friends. She was just entering medical college to start her professional education to become a medical doctor. My mother felt that was an appropriate name for me, as she was hoping that one day her own daughter would also become a medical doctor; a wish that came true.

Sumedha ultimately was an appropriate name, especially because of how the meaning of it is broken down:

Su = Good
Medha = Wisdom (Buddhi)

I later learned that Sumedha is also the name of the leading horse of the chariot of Lord Indra, the celestial God of the Heavens.

So, my life's journey began with:

"A powerful message and blessing from my mother".
"A strong belief in the power of the Divine Feminine."
"A name that also contained a spiritual direction for my life".

Yes, and it has been a great journey that I have pursued with Intention, Determination, Courage, Persistence and Focus.

And in this life, I have been helped, encouraged, and guided by many "Guides" and "Fellow-Travelers".

This Collage of my life contains some glimpses in the form of stories and pictures.

It is great to look at life and feel honored and Joyful about:

A Life Well Lived.

2

My Dancing Feet

I was born with dancing feet.

I think I must have been a dancer in one of my previous lives. As a child, I had a recurring vision of myself as a Celestial Apsara (a beautiful celestial dancer from the Heavens), dressed in light blue, glowing, and flowing attire (a three-piece, special dance costume), adorned with fine jewelry, dancing bells on my ankles, and descending from the sky - dancing.

During my one and only reading with a psychic, whom I had never met before, I was told that she saw me as a dancer wearing a white, decorated attire of the Moghul period, dancing in a Royal Court.

I have never learned formal dancing in a professional dance school. Yet, at age 10 in school in India, I choreographed a group dance guiding the professional musicians.

At age 13, I was selected for a dance-drama performance that was choreographed and directed by dancers and musicians from All India Radio. This was to be presented at a large community function celebrating the Golden Jubilee of our High School. There were 32 students, all girls, in this Dance Drama: two main dancers who played the roles of Hero and Heroine and ten each in the next three rows, selected according to the level of professional dance training and skills they had, to accompany the main dancers in the story that unfolded through the dance-drama. Not having attended a formal dance school, I was placed in the third row, the chorus line. However, when the drums started (Tabla give the dance rhythm in Kathak- North Indian classical dance) my feet automatically moved with the rhythm. As we were wearing dancing bells (Ghungroo) around our ankles, this was promptly noted by the dance director. He called me forward and asked the Tabla player to play different rhythms, and my feet just responded naturally. I couldn't control them. This prompted the dance director to move me to the role of the Heroine of the Play.

When I moved to Lady Hardinge Medical College, during my first year in my studies, another Dance Drama was being organized. The director did not feel that the girl who was chosen to dance one of the two major roles was doing well. Three days before the presentation of this show to the public at our College's Annual Day Function, I was asked to replace that girl and had to learn all the steps in a very short time. I had no problem doing that.

In my third year in medical college, I was elected as the Entertainment President of the College. During our College's Annual Function, we were asked to present some entertainment programs including, dances, plays and songs. I choreographed the "Folk Dances of India" program that consisted of six dances from different geographical and cultural regions of India. I choreographed each one of these dances and taught 60 girls to perform them. I personally took part in three and directed the musicians for the dance show. This was a continuous performance of six dances with no curtain draw between the dances, so I was wearing three different costumes, taking off one after each dance. The musicians were amazed at this dance production. My feet had blisters all over, but nothing could stop me.

In another performance in the medical college annual event, a dance drama story was arranged on the "Light of Asia", a story of Buddha's life when he was meditating under the Bodhi tree. The

Angels wanted to test his concentration and they sent a beautiful celestial dancer to disturb his meditation. I was chosen to be that dancer. When the musicians asked me what rhythm and tune, I wanted them to play, I told them just to play what they thought was appropriate. They began to play, and I just moved into my dance rhythm naturally, never before having heard or practiced this music.

So, yes, I was born with dancing feet. Maybe I also felt deep in my heart that I would take up professional dancing in this life. But this was a different cultural period. I was born in a family where education was given high priority. Dancing or other cultural pursuits, especially for girls (and even for boys), was not considered desirable or worthwhile. Even I felt that I wanted to pursue a professional life as a medical doctor, a surgeon to be precise. And that is what I have pursued in this life's journey.

After I left India in 1962, there were few opportunities for me to continue to dance other than maybe a performance in one of the educational institutions.

Yet, I still dance – whenever the rhythm of Tabla starts anywhere, my feet just automatically and naturally begin to move with the rhythm. Often, I just dance to the rhythm by myself in my home. This is my meditation practice now. This is the way I connect with my Inner-Being.

When I was growing up, we didn't have a camera, so there are very few photographs of me dancing in the events I have mentioned. The few that were taken at the college functions are included in this Journal as glimpses of me as a dancer.

Sumedha Mona Khanna dancing at a function at the School of Publlic Health, University of Pittsburgh, in 1967.

3

Moving On To My Chosen Professional Journey

At age 16, after completing my high school and pre-medical studies, I entered Lady Hardinge Medical College, my alma-mater, in New Delhi, India. This is an all-girls medical college, the only one in the world. The competition was tough to gain entrance. Only 50 new students were admitted through an all-India competition with a written and oral examination. Of these, 25 were selected: 2 from each State, through a Statewide competition. Twenty-five others were selected from an open all-India competition. Since Delhi was not a State, I had to compete for one of these open places. I stood seventh in that competition, so I gained admission to this prestigious and very high-quality medical college.

Studying comes to me naturally. I am focused and love to study with no distraction, sometimes even forgetting to eat.

Almost all my teachers were women, this after all was an all-girls educational institution. The few men who worked here were in the non-clinical teaching positions, such as pharmacology, toxicology, anatomy, and physiology.

At this phase of my professional life, I didn't have to compete with boys, or be distracted by them. This was a journey with fellow-girls, under the mentorship of some remarkable women teachers, each one an exemplary leader in her own field.

Unquestionably, this was a Woman's World. Being with some of the most courageous and brilliant classmates, as well as those who had entered the College earlier than me, gave me an environment in which to grow fearlessly and with clear foresight for my own future. These were girls who had left their homes, families, and cultural environment for higher studies, to pursue professional careers. As many had come from different regions of India and spoke different languages, English became our common language for communication. We all adopted different cultural traditions to become one common culture, The Hardonian Culture, where there was no enmity or cultural bias. We had healthy competition to excel in our studies, while supporting each other.

Among the girls in my class and beyond, those who stand out in my memory include Adarsh Jain; Kamlesh Sharma/Dada; Krishna Chowdhary/Taneja; Susheela Chauhan, we called her LC; Raj Popli, with whom I always competed in studies; Usha (Sabharwal/Nayar; Anjali Saha; and many others.

There were also many very capable teachers who were exemplary in their knowledge and ability. They inculcated great values in us, values of service to the community, dedication to our patients, and of course excellence in knowledge. Among them, the following stand out in my memory:

Dr. S. Achaya – Professor of Anatomy
Dr. Parvati Malkani – Professor of Obstetrics/Gynecology
Dr. Ansuya Dass - Professor of Obstetrics and Gynecology
Dr. S. Chowdhury – Professor of Surgery
Dr. Sumedha Pathak – Professor of Internal Medicine
Dr. Padmavati – Professor of Internal Medicine

It is interesting that most of these women never married. They were intelligent women who excelled in their chosen specialty. They were great teachers and mentors, dedicated to their profession. These were strong women of the "Gandhian period", and I believe they had a very important influence on my professional career, values, and character.

4

Seeking Higher And Specialized Professional Education

Leaving India

I completed my medical education in India in 1960, at age 20 1/2 years. After completing the mandatory one-year Internship, I graduated formally in 1961. I was just 21 1/2 years old.

I wanted to pursue higher postgraduate studies to specialize in obstetrics and gynecology. At that time, India, being a recent independent country from England, had not developed higher professional education institutions. The only opportunity for specialized higher medical education for me was to go to either Madras (now Chennai) in the south, specifically, or to England. My parents were very interested in higher education for their children. They agreed to send me to England, where my elder brother had gone for higher education already and had settled there with his family. My parents felt that at least there would be some family support for me in the beginning.

Even though the idea of my marriage came to my mother's mind, she did not put any pressure on me. She knew that I was totally against that, and my father supported me in that.

In March 1962, before I was 23, I left India for England, with one suitcase, a small carry-on bag, a medical degree, and 3 British pounds and ten shillings (the only foreign exchange amount that we were allowed in those days), my heart full of blessings from my parents and great anticipation for my professional career. I took the BOAC (British Oversees Airway Corporation) flight to London and was met by my brother Inder upon arrival.

Pursuing Higher Education in England 1962-1966

Entering a New Culture and in A Man's World

I arrived in London in March 1962. By early April, I got my first job as a substitute junior resident in Surgery at Bedford General Hospital. This was a three-month assignment that included covering a Casualty Department (24-hour emergency clinic). Bedford is an industrial town north of London, close to Motorway 1, the main highway from London to north England. Many vehicle accidents occurred on this motorway and so the Casualty Department was always very busy, especially at nights.

This was my first exposure to emergency surgical care, and I found that I really liked it. I had no apprehension. I had plenty of courage to deal with patients who were brought in, sometimes with major trauma. Of course, I was working under a very capable senior resident and the surgeon (Dr. Bernard Cashmann). I also discovered that I was good at surgical techniques. My supervisors were very impressed with my precision and dexterity. This early demonstration of my surgical skills and focus carried me forward to my professional career. I developed self-confidence and acquired praise and recognition from my supervisors.

All my supervisors and seniors were men. The only women at the hospital were nurses, other than one other Indian junior resident in obstetrics and gynecology department. Yes, there was some dominance and superiority among the male supervisors, who were all English and white.

An interesting incident comes to mind, when I went for my first interview for a job in one of the hospitals in London (prior to getting the substitute job in Bedford Hospital). I was ushered into a room full of white, elderly (they all seemed so, as I was so young and petite) gentlemen. They saw a petite young girl (5 ft. 2 "), thin (100 lbs.), and Indian, who didn't even look like a medical doctor. I certainly didn't fit their image of what a medical doctor should look like. They were surprised at my youth and the fact that I had graduated from medical college before I was 21. And no, I did not get selected for this job, possibly because I was young, and maybe even because I was a young woman.

Even in Bedford, I occasionally felt this sense of superiority and dominance among the male doctors and sometimes even from nurses who were mostly white and much older than me. Most of them couldn't pronounce my name, Sumedha, so they preferred to call me by my nickname, Mona. And because of my family name, Khanna, some of them began to call me Jim (for Gymkhana). I was quite amused by this and just went along with it. I didn't feel offended or dominated by this; I thought it was funny. I was secure in myself. Even though, in retrospect, I think it was quite colonial and a sign of those individuals feeling superior, at that time, I was fresh from a newly independent country of the colonial British, so their attitudes were not surprising. It didn't take long for me to demonstrate my skills and attention to detail. This, as well as my get-along personality with my colleagues and very attentive patient care, earned me their respect.

Yes, I had to earn their acceptance and respect. It didn't come as automatically as it probably would have if I had been an English man starting on a higher professional journey.

This is when I learned the **First Lessons** of being a woman in a Man's World. Compound this with the fact that I also happened to be from a developing country (called Third-World country those days), working in a First-World country, that had a 'Colonial' attitude.

Here are those lessons I learned, summed up:

1. **The only way to earn their acceptance and respect is through a demonstration of your skills and ability.**

2. **Learn to go along with their sense of humor and superiority, while staying focused, not getting overwhelmed, and without showing inferiority.**

3. **Don't question or try to change them. Keep your head down and remain focused on your goals and quest for your own future (in which they will not have a place).**

4. **Remain focused on acquiring more knowledge and skills, always.**

5. **Advance professionally, despite them. You don't have to become like them.**

6. **Learn all you can from those who have skills and knowledge, without developing their bad attitudes.**

I feel that at least in the professional medical world, eventually it is your skills, knowledge, and the way you handle your patients and any situation that you encounter, that make you an equal partner and colleague. But it takes time, so as a woman, keep your head down and stay focused on your goal.

There was not much talk about Gender discrimination in these times. I was in a world of professionals, and I had to be one of them. I also learned that once you are a medical doctor, you are automatically respected.

My Professional Journey In England

1. 1962, April – June:
    - Junior (substitute) Resident in Surgery and Emergency clinic at Bedford General Hospital
2. 1963, June - December:
    - Junior Obstetrics/Gynecology Resident in Elizabeth Garrett Anderson (a branch of the Royal Free Hospital) in London
3. 1963, January – March:
    - Senior Ob/Gyn Resident in North Middlesex Hospital, London
    - Obtained Diploma in OB/Gyn from the Royal College of Ob/Gyn England (D.R.C.O.G.)
4. 1963, April – September:
    - Senior Ob/Gyn Resident in Queen Mary's Hospital for East End, London
5. 1963 - 1965, October 1963 - September 1965:
    - Senior Resident/Registrar in Ob/Gyn, Epsom District Hospital, Epsom, Surrey
    - Passed the exam for Membership Ob/Gyn of the Royal College of England (MRCOG)
6. 1965, September-December:
    - Senior Resident (substitute) in Surgery/Emergency Dept., Lewisham Hospital, London
7. 1966, December-March:
    - Consultant Ob/Gyn (substitute), Epsom District Hospital, Epsom, Surrey

Some Glimpses And Anecdotes Of My Professional Life In England

Elizabeth Garrett Hospital, London[2]:

Here, I was once again in a Woman's World, for six months of residency in Ob/Gyn. This Hospital for Women opened the path for me to pursue my specialization in Obstetrics and Gynecology.

Elizabeth Garrett Anderson (9 June 1836 - 17 December 1917) was an English Physician and Suffragette, the second English woman to qualify as a physician and surgeon in Britain in 1865. She was the co-founder of the first hospital staffed by women in 1899, named the Elizabeth Garrett Anderson Hospital. She was the first Dean of a British Medical School and the first female Doctor of Medicine in France. She in fact was the first Woman officially approved to practice medicine in Great Britain. She made great sacrifices and struggled to create new pathways for women in British Medicine.

It was my good fortune that brought me to this hospital. I applied for a job of junior resident in Obstetrics/Gynecology, advertised in the British Journal of Obstetrics and Gynecology. My supervisor surgeon in Bedford General Hospital (Dr. Bernard Cashman) gave a glorious reference for me (even though I never saw it). When I was interviewed by the senior Ob/Gyn Consultant (Ms. Mocata) of the hospital, she told me that she had received an excellent reference from Dr. Cashman and would appoint me for the job based on that. I was over the moon to have gained my first Ob/Gyn job in such a historic and prestigious hospital. It was also a branch of the Royal Free Hospital, a very prestigious teaching hospital in London.

When I joined this hospital, there were three women Ob/Gyn Specialists/Consultants: Miss Mocata; Miss Josephine Barnes; and Ms. Elizabeth Hunter. (In England, once a physician passes the MRCOG exam and thus officially becomes a Member of The Royal College of Obstetricians and Gynecologists, he/she earns the title of a Mr. or Ms., considered to be higher than a Dr., as it represents specialization. An interesting fact!). I was assigned as the junior house-surgeon under Ms. Mocata, and I also worked under Ms.

Josephine Barnes. I must have felt the spirit of Elizabeth Garrett Anderson that dwelt in this hospital. The dedication, quality, and compassion that these women physicians provided to this hospital were palpable. I am sure that I inherited this spirit. All physicians and patients in this hospital were women. I was a fast learner, and these women were great teachers and mentors.

The only exception was one of the senior residents, Elizabeth Tooth, a tall white woman. At times, she served as my senior advisor and was very dominating with what I would call a 'Colonial' attitude, at times abusive. I think being a white tall English woman, she felt superior, especially to a short Indian physician from a post-colonial country. However, I was not afraid. I did not feel subservient. I stood up to her through my skills, details of attention, and stopped her from using abusive language.

My two Consultants/Supervisors, Ms. Mocata and Ms. Josephine Barnes, supported me and gave me much freedom in my work. In fact, due to my sharp wit and attention that once saved the life of a woman, a private patient of Ms. Barnes, the latter never forgot that. She not only gave me great references for my future job applications, but also personally reached out to consultants who interviewed me for these jobs.

Ms. Josephine Barnes was later honored by
Queen Elizabeth and given the title of Dame Josephine Barnes.

Onward to a male-dominated hospital:
Queen Mary's Hospital for the East End [3]

Queen Mary's Hospital for East End (1861-1983) was a historic hospital in the East End of London, that started as a dispensary in 1861 by a local doctor. It became the oldest voluntary hospital in West Ham and a had a long history of serving the community. It was in this historic and prestigious hospital that I was selected as the Senior Resident in OB/Gyn. There were two Consultants in OB/Gyn, Mr. Spiers and Mr. Methuen. I was assigned to the Senior Consultant, Mr. Spiers. A junior resident, an Irishman, was assigned to Mr. Methuen.

I was interviewed only by Mr. Methuen, the junior consultant, who had received excellent references of my work in the Elizabeth Garrett Anderson Hospital. Mr. Spiers, the senior consultant, had not met me before my appointment. Next day during my first hospital round, I met Mr. Spiers for the first time. He looked at me with big surprise. "Oh! You are the new Senior House Surgeon. Wow! You are so small, you won't be able to pull a baby out!", he said. I looked straight at him and said, "Sir, you can rest assured that I won't use excessive force in pulling a baby out." Mr. Spiers was quite surprised at my response. He didn't expect a young female doctor from India to be so bold. No further comment from me. I had encountered the 'Colonial' attitudes for the second time in my professional journey in England.

During my six-month residency, I did not take one night or day off, as the junior Resident was not very confident. He was an older, Irish doctor who didn't like Obstetrics, but as he wanted to qualify to be a General Family Practitioner, he had to do a mandatory 6-months Residency in Obstetrics/Gynecology. I told him not to worry, as I would be there to support him. During these six months, I took on more and more responsibility and became very confident and skilled in Ob/Gyn. work. Even though a couple of times Mr. Spiers tried to belittle me, I stood up to him and he eventually became very impressed with my skills, decision-making ability, and courage. Once, I even had the opportunity to do a life-saving surgery on one of his patients (since he was too inebriated with alcohol to perform). Toward the end of my assignment, he even invited me to his prestigious Harley Street Surgery office. He praised my work and gave me an excellent reference. H even invited me to work with him in his private practice, which I declined.

While at Queen Mary's Hospital, I also passed my exam in Diploma in Ob/Gyn of the Royal College of Obstetricians and Gynecologists. This was a first step toward specialization. I gained a lot of respect from my colleagues, all of whom were white English men.

> (*Noteworthy- I was working in this hospital when the assassination of President Kennedy was announced.*)

Epsom District Hospital [4]

My assignment in Epsom District Hospital as Registrar in Ob/Gyn was from 1964-1966.

Here were two Ob/Gyn teams, each with a Consultant, Registrar (senior resident) and a House-Surgeon (junior resident). I was assigned to one of these teams. My consultant was very pleasant, and eager to teach and pass on his skills to his juniors. A thorough English gentleman who had a big country house, although I was never invited to it. The British generally are very reticent about inviting people, especially foreigners to their homes. He had a very cultured and sophisticated wife, and he loved to play golf. My junior house-surgeon was also a very white Englishman, a bit harsh. I think he respected me because I was his boss but, deep inside, I think he felt a bit of hostility. Three incidents confirmed my impression.

The first one was when a young unmarried English girl, full term pregnant, arrived as an emergency at the hospital, with very embarrassed parents. My junior resident met them and admitted her to the labor ward. He didn't inform me. After she had been in labor for several hours with no progress, he had to call me. I checked her condition; she was very exhausted and the baby's heart rate was getting very high. Since her labor hadn't progressed, the only option was to do a Cesarean section. I ordered the preparation of the Operation Theatre, yet there was uneasiness in me. I was not certain that I could clearly define the baby's head and it was definitely not engaged. So, in the middle of this emergency, in the operating theatre, I ordered an x-ray of the young girl's abdomen. My junior resident and some of the nursing staff were very concerned that delay would endanger the baby's life, but they reluctantly followed my order. My instinct was proven right. The x-ray showed that the baby's head was not fully formed, a case of Anencephaly, and that the baby wouldn't have survived anyway. I informed the parents of the situation and advised that we should induce labor to let her deliver normally. They agreed. In fact, they felt relieved that their young daughter wouldn't have to have surgery, a scar she would carry the rest of her life, and that the baby would be born dead. Eventually, she delivered a still-born baby. Everyone was relieved and I think I gained respect from all my colleagues.

The second incident was when a general practitioner, who was taking care of his private patient's delivery at her home, felt that the labor was not progressing and called my junior resident. According to the hospital protocol, he should have called me, the senior resident. However, when he learned that not only was I a woman, but also an Indian (foreigner), he felt embarrassed to call me first.

When I arrived at the patient's house, I didn't show any anger. I simply proceeded to examine the patient and found out that it was a breach (the baby's bottom was coming out first). A breach delivery can be tricky and should be taken care of at the hospital. I quietly informed the General Practitioner that what he was looking at was not the baby's head, but the baby's bottom and that we should transfer the patient to the hospital. I let him explain the situation to the family, who agreed.

In the hospital I also found out, when delivering the baby, that it had a spina-bifida (split in the spine) and a hydrocephalic head, that had to be drained through the spinal split. The baby of course was still born. It was a sad and unfortunate incident, but everyone was grateful and relieved that the woman was O.K.

I think I earned the respect of the general practitioner and, through him, the rest of the other General Practitioners. Epsom was a small town where people knew each other, and gossip got around.

My consultant, when he heard about it, gave me a high complement.

The third incident happened when another General Practitioner was delivering his patient in the hospital. The patient was getting exhausted and the G.P. decided to deliver the baby with forceps, a recommended procedure. When he couldn't manage that, he called my junior resident for help (once again a breach of protocol). The two of them together couldn't budge the baby's head. They then called me for help.

I went to the labor ward and delivered the baby with the forceps within 3 minutes. The mother and the baby were fine, but the two guys, both 6 ft. tall and big, were surprised that I had so much more strength than the two of them together. "How did you do that?", they asked. "It is not a question of force, rather the tactic. You forgot to rotate the head."

I continued to earn the respect of that very English and male community through demonstration of my skills, patience, and compassion. Many older women patients, who came to the hospital for gynecological problems, recognized that and trusted me. In fact, even asked for me whenever they came. They liked the idea of being seen by a woman doctor and felt freer to talk about their problems. I don't think male physicians are that sensitive. Many of my patients gave me gifts, but most of all I loved being honored and appreciated by them.

My consultant recognized these qualities, too, and continued to give me more and more freedom for decision-making, about the patients' situation and for surgery. Within two years of my assignment there, I became a proficient Ob/Gyn practitioner and passed my MRCOG exam (Membership of the Royal College of Obstetricians and Gynecologists) at my first attempt, a very rare thing that led to even higher respect for me among my colleagues and hospital staff. Once you become a Member of the Royal College of Ob/Gyn, you are considered a specialist and can qualify for a higher level, even a consultant position, in a hospital, or go into private practice.

The senior resident in the other Ob/Gyn team, an Irishman who was much older and had already attempted the MRCOG exam at least three times, had not yet passed the exam. That of course created a bit of jealousy, but overall, he was a light-hearted and pleasant person and respected me.

An important and telling compliment that I received from my consultant's wife was that ever since I joined his team, he hadn't been called, even once, at night in two years and had not missed a round of golf.

In 1965, I completed my OB/Gyn Residency and passed the Member of The Royal College of Obstetricians/Gynecologists (MRCOG) specialist examination. I still had another six months of my Residency program at the Epsom District Hospital.

The word of my proficiency somehow got around, and I was approached by the Royal College of OB/Gyn, to consider specializing in Female Cancer Surgery. I was known to be an excellent surgeon, having performed many cesarean sections, hysterectomies, and other more complex vaginal surgeries. I was also known for having very good manual dexterity. So, my supervisors agreed that I was a good candidate for female cancer surgery, a specialty just advancing due to better surgical techniques. I was offered a full scholarship by the Royal Society of Medicine.

One of the requirements was to take the exam for the Fellowship of the Royal College of Surgeons (FRCS). Studying for exams was always a passion for me. I knew that I could focus and study and was quite capable of passing another exam. It seemed an exciting and unique opportunity for me, a young doctor from India, a woman just 26 years old with a whole professional life ahead of me. So, I accepted the challenge and the offer, and began to study for my exam. Part one was mainly a detailed anatomy. I was already very good in anatomy, having received a Distinction in the subject in my second year in Medical College, as well as the prize for the best dissection. By this time, I was a senior resident in my second year. I was given a beautiful apartment near the hospital where I had my own kitchen that allowed me to cook and meet some friends. I also bought my first car, after having passed my driver's exam in the first attempt, another rarity those days.

The future looked promising. I was single, unattached, with an occasional male friend here and there, and had no interest in marriage, or even in a serious affair. I did not want any interruption in my professional life. My parents were very proud of me and were hoping that I would return to India soon.

5

A Change in Direction

In March of 1966, just three months away from the end of my posting as a Registrar in Epsom District Hospital, something extraordinary happened to me, while studying for the FRCS exam in my flat in the hospital. I remember this very clearly. It was March 9, 1966. I was holding the femur bone of the skeleton that I had in my room (whom I had given the name Jimmy). I was studying the attachments to this bone, in the area called Linea Aspera, realized that I already knew this, and began to wonder why I was studying it again.

Then something flashed through my mind - the images of women, who had come to Lady Hardinge Hospital, generally in the late stages of cancer, when surgery was not an option. Chemotherapy had not been developed yet, at least in India. The only thing we could offer was palliative care, with pain relieving medications and radium needles inserted in the cancerous growth (if that was an option still feasible) to reduce the size. Most of the time that didn't work well. I recalled taking care of a woman with vaginal cancer and inserting radium needles in her growth. I was not wearing any protective gear myself. Within 6 months, my white blood cell count came down and I was then removed from this duty. The damage must have been done by then - I have no idea.

Another image flashed through my mind - that of women being brought to the maternity emergency ward with prolonged labor, exhausted. Sometimes the fetal heart rate was not even discernible. Sometimes the baby was born dead; occasionally the woman also did not survive. When asked why it took so long to bring her to hospital, no one could give a specific answer. The family just thought that the situation would be resolved in time. Sometimes there was no suitable transportation available to bring the woman and the accompanying family members.

I began to ask the question:" Why do women die at childbirth?"

Something shifted in my consciousness at this moment. Why was I considering specializing in Female Cancer Surgery, when I realized that I would end up working in either a Tertiary Care Hospital or a Teaching Hospital, super-specialized in Female Cancer Surgery, in a large city, as there weren't many such highly specialized hospitals in India at that time.

I felt that my aim was to serve many women, to try to prevent maternal death and reduce infant mortality. I knew that it was not the lack of technology that could prevent their suffering or death. Rather, it was the social environment in which the mother and children lived, the poverty, and the fact that women generally had no power to make decisions about their health or their bodies. I felt that I needed to learn more about the social aspects of Obstetrics and Gynecology and social determinants of maternal health.

I threw Jimmy's femur away and went to the Hospital library. There, I started checking up books on Social and Preventive Medicine/Public Health Programs. I had very little knowledge about this, so I started researching the Public Health Schools that offered Maternal and Child Health Specialty. In England, there was just one Public Health School, the London School of Tropical Hygiene (it was called at that time), that only offered a Diploma Program on Tropical Medicine. This was not my objective.

Coincidently, in February, I had attended a lecture at the Royal Society of Medicine in London, delivered by a visiting, American professor, who was the Dean of the University of Pittsburgh

Medical School. He was the cousin of a colleague of mine, so I was personally introduced to him. The visiting professor and his wife wanted to have dinner at the famous Mirabelle Restaurant in London. My friend and I took them there, and we enjoyed a delicious meal and a very interesting evening. Then he told me that if I ever wanted to come to the USA, I should think of Pittsburgh.

So, I started looking for information about the School of Public Health in Pittsburgh. I found that it was a very progressive school, just starting an extended Maternal and Child Health Program, with a specialty in Population Control.

It is important to note that the 1960's was the pioneer decade for Family Planning. Improvement in health, declining infant and child mortality, combined with high birth rates in many newly independent countries, gave rise to the concern that this would create high pressure on available resources, as well as on health services. With the International Planned Parenthood Federation (IPPF) leading research and testing new contraceptive methods, the Intrauterine Contraception Device (IUD) and the Oral Contraceptive Pill were added to the traditional methods, such as condoms and the Diaphragm and Rhythm method. I took special training at the IPPF London Clinic, where I was almost the first, fully qualified Ob/Gyn specialist with complete training in contraception, family planning methods, and counseling.

At this time, I also decided to take the Educational Council for Foreign Medical Graduates (ECFMG) exam. This was requisite for being accepted in a medical training facility, in the USA. I passed this exam in my first attempt.

In March 1966, I wrote to the Dean of the School of Public Health, University of Pittsburgh (I did not know his name) to indicate my interest in pursuing a Master's in Public Health (MPH), with a major in Maternal and Child Health and Population Dynamics. I was surprised to receive a response within two weeks that there was positive interest in my application. The University had just received some funds, from a Private Foundation, for scholarships to foreign students from developing countries. I would qualify for this, provided I had sponsorship from my Government (India). The University also enclosed application forms.

I sent my application along with recommendations from my previous supervisors in the UK. I also informed the acting Dean, who was at that time Dr. Samuel Wishik, that I could not produce my government's sponsorship, as it didn't know of my existence. I had been pursuing my higher education and supporting myself so far, however, would appreciate receiving a scholarship.

Introducing Dr. Samuel Wishik

A few words about Dr. Samuel Wishik (generally called Sam Wishik) who appeared in my life at this crucial transition phase- merely an accident- and without him I wouldn't have moved forward in my professional life as I did. He literally provided the steppingstone as well as became my mentor counsellor and Guide for this phase of my professional life. Dr. Wishik was the head of the Maternal and Child Health Division of the Pittsburgh School of Public Health. He had gone on a two-year assignment in Pakistan on a Population Control/Family Planning Mission with the Ford Foundation. He had recently returned from this mission to the University and was acting Dean of the School of Public Health when my letter arrived. What a coincidence! I am sure if the actual Dean was there my application may not have received the attention that it did.
(More about Dr. Wishik later as my life proceeds.

By early April, I received an Acceptance Letter from the University of Pittsburgh along with an offer of scholarship from the Mellon Foundation that would cover my tuition, lodging and books/

supplies etc. It was a generous scholarship. All I had to provide was my travel cost to USA. I could easily afford that.

I prepared myself to leave for USA. I completed my assignment in Epsom District Hospital at the end of June. During July-August, I was offered several short-term locum positions (relieving someone on holiday) including a two-week locum as a Consultant in Epsom District Hospital as substitute for Mr. Gordon who was my boss and was taking a 2-week vacation. This was an unusual honor for a young Indian doctor just 27 years old and acting as a consultant in a posh very British hospital. Vow! I had earned the ultimate recognition at the end of my stay in England.

Onward to the USA

In August 1966, I took a boat from Southampton to New York, the airlines were on strike, and shared a cabin with a young American girl from Ohio. We were four young women, three Americans and I, sharing a table in the dining room. We got to know each other well and enjoyed our journey. As a medical doctor, I was especially invited to a cocktail party given by the Ship's doctor, a tradition on the British Cruise ship. My group was surprised to learn that not only I was a young Indian woman, but also a doctor. Another incidence of *A Woman in a Man's World.*

IN PITTSBURGH

AUGUST 1966 – JUNE 1967
PERSUING MASTER'S DEGREE IN PUBLIC HEALTH

I arrived in Pittsburgh via Washington D.C., where I had stopped for a couple of days to visit an old colleague from India. He was a senior resident in Surgery, and I was working as a junior resident with him at the Irwin Hospital. He had moved to the USA and stayed in touch with me, as he was interested in marriage with me. However, I was neither ready, nor interested, and was able to tell him about this during my visit so there wouldn't be any such expectation in the future. Of course, he was disappointed, but for me, that was the end of the story and I proceeded to Pittsburgh, on a Greyhound bus.

I was met by the Secretary of the Dean. She had already found an apartment for me. I had no car, but the apartment was close to a tram terminal that could take me to the School.

Next day I visited Dr. Wishik, the acting Dean of the School. He was in the hospital for some procedure I believe. He still welcomed me warmly and introduced his very pleasant secretary, Ms. Louise, who helped me a great deal in settling down and in orientation. I also learned that one of my doctor colleagues from London, who had become a close friend during our assignment in a hospital, had moved to Pittsburgh to pursue his Fellowship in Surgery. This turned out to be very helpful. Our friendship became closer and more cordial (although not romantic or with any intention of pursuing marriage).

My studies in Pittsburgh went smoothly. I found the course materials easy to follow. The whole education system was different in the USA, requiring a lot of self-study and responsibility for oneself.

We had excellent professors. I learned to use the library and developed better writing skills. This was a time before computers, so I also learned to use the typewriter, but just with two-finger typing.

There were nine students in the Population cohort, including me, Tony Gold (a young American woman from New York), a young woman from Burma, an older woman doctor from Pittsburgh (medical director of the City Health Department), an Indian doctor from Canada, an older physician from Ireland, and a couple of others. We formed a very congenial group. Dr. Wishik, our supervisor, encouraged a lot of self-study and open learning.

The year went very fast. I graduated in June 1967, first in the class, so I was designated as Class Marshall. Thus, I was given the honor to lead the class at the commencement ceremony. I wore a white saree and felt very proud, wishing of course that this was witnessed by some member of my family.

The school had a tradition that the foreign students were assigned a 3-month internship, after graduation, in a local health department. However, I was approached by the Dean to take an assignment in Jamaica, West Indies, where the School was engaged in developing a School of Preventive Medicine, at the University of the West Indies, with a past student, Dr. Kenneth Standard. The School was also conducting a Family Planning, Knowledge, Attitude and Practice (KAP), Study in the neighboring community. This was a special request and of course I enthusiastically agreed. Little did I know that this would lead to a major change in the direction of my professional journey.

6

Onward To An Unknown Professional Journey

Let it Unfold

Moving to Jamaica

In June 1967, I moved to Jamaica for a six-month assignment with the University of the West Indies (UWI). Another student from Pittsburgh, Toni Gold, also joined me for a 3-month Internship. We rented rooms in a house owned by a Jamaican Nurse/Midwife, Ms. Maynard, who worked at the University. It is interesting that the name of the University's campus in Kingston is MONA, which is my middle name. Toni and I bought a second-hand car to help us get around.

During my stay in Jamaica, I worked as a Research Associate with the Dept. of Social and Preventive Medicine, UWI, working with Prof. Kenneth Standard (head of the Dept., who had recently graduated from the University of Pittsburgh School of Public Health), and Dr. Karl Smith. I think the University of Pittsburgh's association with UWI, specifically the Department of Social and Preventive Medicine, began with Prof. Standard becoming the head of the Dept. I participated in a KAP (Knowledge, Attitude and Practice) survey in Family Planning that was being carried out in two areas served by the UWI. I also worked at the Victoria Jubilee Hospital in Kingston, with Dr. Williams- the Director of the National Family Planning Program. This Program was beginning to launch various Family Planning activities, including establishing Family Planning Clinics in the entire country within the health centers.

During this time, Dr. Wishik moved to Columbia University's Institute for the Study of Human Reproduction. Dr. John Cutler, who was the Assistant Director of The Pan American Health Organization, PAHO, moved to the University of Pittsburgh, replacing Dr. Wishik, as Head of the Department of Public Health. So technically, I had to report to Dr. Cutler, as he was now my supervisor at the School of Public Health, yet I continued my consultation and association with Dr. Wishik.

I became involved in training physicians in Family Planning techniques, especially in the insertion of the Intrauterine Device, a very new procedure. I was one of the few medical doctors trained in this by the distinguished Margaret Sanger Institute in London. At this time, few physicians were trained or familiar with this procedure, at all. Dr. Wishik continued to advise me on technical and administrative procedures. I worked in many health centers on the Island, starting family planning clinics within the rural health centers. I also connected with the International Planned Parenthood Directors in Jamaica. During this period of my assignment, I also participated in some family planning activities in St. Vincent and Barbados.

At this time, both Dr. Wishik and I began to contact the Government of India's Ministry of Health and several agencies, including The Ford Foundation, USAID, and Population Council, to explore job possibilities for me in India. I was still interested in returning to India to work there and be with my parents, helping them in their advancing years. My father was about to retire, and I wanted to take care of them. But, I didn't receive any response from India. I was offered the opportunity of working in Jamaica and Barbados, as an Ob/Gyn practitioner, both in the Government service and in private practice, but I did not really want to settle in the Caribbean, so far from India.

I was not surprised at not receiving any encouraging response from India. It was too bureaucratic, and I didn't personally know anyone there to get a recommendation. I then approached the WHO's Geneva Office. The response I received was that I needed to have at least five years of experience in Public Health before it would even consider an application. Dr. Wishik, too, offered me a job, as a Research Associate under him at Columbia University, New York, for after my assignment ended in Jamaica.

A Coincidence Or Higher Intervention

At this time, another event took place that changed the direction of my professional life. The first intervention was in March 1966, when I received an "internal" direction to move from Clinical OB/Gyn to Social aspects of women's health that led to my move to Pittsburgh to pursue studies in Public Health and obtain my master's degree. In September 1967, a second intervention occurred that changed the direction of my professional life completely and took me to places that I could never have imagined, earlier in my career.

Latin America held its First Population Conference in Caracas, Venezuela, to discuss the introduction of Family Planning/Population Control Programs in various countries. This was attended by the heads of many International Agencies involved in Population Control/ Family Planning Programs, including: International Planned Parenthood Federation (IPPF); Population Council, New York; US Agency for International Development (USAID), and WHO, represented by Dr. Abraham Horwitz, Director of the Pan American Health Organization (PAHO). PAHO also served as the Regional Office of WHO, for the American Region. Dr. Wishik and Dr. John Cutler also attended this Conference.

At this Conference, Dr. Wishik met with Dr. Max Avon, the Minister of Health of Trinidad and Tobago, who informed him that Trinidad and Tobago were just starting a National Family Planning Program. It had established a Population Council, which included representatives from the Ministry of Health, Government Policy/Political Leadership, IPPF, represented by the Family Planning Association of Trinidad and Tobago, and Catholic Marriage Advisory Council of Trinidad and Tobago. The Minister requested the services of a Technical Consultant in Family Planning, who would train the Ministry's appointed head of the National Family Planning Program and help in designing the National Family Planning Program. So, the idea came up that I would be assigned to Trinidad and Tobago under the aegis of the Institute for the Study of Human Reproduction, Columbia University, New York, and Dr. Wishik would serve as the advisor. Dr. Wishik suggested that I travel to some of the countries in Asia to observe their Family Planning Programs, with the appointed head of Trinidad and Tobago's National Family Planning Program. When he/she came to the USA for MPH studies in 1968, I would remain in Trinidad in charge of the National FP Program, until the end of 1969, and then return to Columbia University to continue my work there. Dr. Wishik also envisioned me as working with some of the countries in the Caribbean and Latin America.

Dr. Cutler, who had also attended this Conference, got involved in discussions with Dr. Avon, Minister of Health, for Trinidad and Tobago, as well. His past connection with PAHO as its Deputy Director led to the possibility of my being assigned to Trinidad as a PAHO/WHO Consultant. Eventually, after further discussions, it was decided that I would be employed as a PAHO/WHO consultant on Family Planning/Population Dynamics in Trinidad, under PAHO's Zone 1 Office, starting in March 1968. The Institute in Columbia University supported this decision with a financial contribution toward my 2-year contract with PAHO. Dr. Wishik informed me of this arrangement through a long hand-written letter from Caracas to Jamaica, where I was completing my assignment from the University of Pittsburgh and preparing to return to New York to start my new assignment at the Institute for the Study of Human Reproduction, Columbia University. In fact, a decision was being made about my future move even before I joined the University. On hindsight, this seems an incredible coincidence of events that nobody, especially me, could have envisaged. In *astrological terms it might be considered as an interplay of planetary influence!!*

Later that year I was introduced to Dr. Horwitz, during the annual Conference of the American Public Health Association (APHA) in Miami, Florida. I was standing between the very tall Dr. John Cutler (6'4") and Dr. Sam Wishik (5'10"). I was only 5'2", 100 lbs., and wearing a blue minidress. Dr. Horwitz's first reaction upon seeing me was, *"Such a little Girl!".* My response was, "I just look little". I was only 28 years old, about to embark on a completely unchartered course of my professional journey, in a country I knew very little about, and had never visited.

I moved to Columbia University in October of 1967, while all these discussions were going on, and then visited India in January 1968 for the first time since I had left, as a special gift to my father on his birthday on January 26, 1968. My father had just turned 58, almost close to his retirement. My parents, although disappointed that I was not returning to India yet, felt very proud of my going to work with WHO, in an international life. My father had never been interested in my working with the Government of India, as he himself had all his life, and was never truly rewarded for his dedicated work and achievement. He always felt that the Government was full of bureaucrats who were incompetent and often corrupt.

I returned to New York in March and made arrangement for my departure to Port of Spain, Trinidad. Prior to that, I visited the PAHO Regional Office, in Washington D.C., to meet with Dr. Abraham Horwitz, Director of PAHO and other senior staff, as well as the

Personnel Department. Dr. Wishik suggested that I wear a Sari to assist me look a bit older. I was only 28 years old, the youngest medical officer in PAHO and WHO ever appointed, and a woman. There were hardly any women in technical professional posts in PAHO and WHO (there were a few at lower professional levels in the Personnel and Financial departments). I was interviewed by mostly older white or Latin American men, Deputy Director and Division Chiefs, who were all skeptical as well as curious about me being appointed to such an important and unique position (first in the field of Family Planning in PAHO and WHO). But I felt that Dr. Horwitz was impressed by me and willing to take the risk.

Before I move further in my life's story, I want to recall the incredibly important role that Dr. Samuel Wishik played in my professional life.

He was the head of the Department of Maternal and Child Health/Population Dynamics at the Graduate School of Public Health, University of Pittsburgh.

When I sent my application/Letter of my intention to pursue my master's in public health, he was acting Dean of the School. What a coincidence! He had recently returned from Pakistan, where he spent a two-year assignment in Family Planning, a program funded by USAID. He was therefore very motivated and energized about the need to introduce family planning in the developing countries. Under his initiative and leadership, the School of Public Health just started a new Graduate Program called Health and Population Dynamics. He was, by nature, more open and less bureaucratic, and sent a very encouraging and positive response to my Letter of Intention.

When I sent my formal application for the Graduate Program, indicating that I would not have my Government (Indian) sponsorship as I had been pursuing my studies independently, he managed to get funding from Foundations (Mellon and Ford) to support scholarships for international students for this new Graduate Program. I was offered a scholarship to cover the cost of my tuition and room and board in Pittsburgh. All I had to pay was my travel from London to Pittsburgh, USA.

He was an excellent teacher and mentor for his students, very approachable, receptive, and encouraging. I recognized him as my Mentor, my first mentor in Public Health. He was open-minded and creatively expansive in his ideas. The fact that he stepped out of boundaries that educational institutions usually present, not only played a major role in charting my future professional career in Public Health, but also helped provide the initial funding to PAHO/WHO for my first assignment in Trinidad and Tobago and the Caribbean. This opened the door to a totally unexpected professional journey in International Health.

Dr. Samuel Wishik became my Mentor for life, continuing to monitor my professional journey, as well as advising me as I needed. He passed away in 2007, at the age of 93.

7

Embarking On An International Health Career

March 1968-November 1993

My twenty-five-year Professional Journey in International Health with the World Health Organization.

March 1968 - August 1970
Served as PAHO/WHO Advisor in Maternal-Child Health and Population Dynamics for the Caribbean countries and Venezuela (PAHO Zone 1 countries), Stationed in Port of Spain, Trinidad.

August 1970 – September 1973
PAHO/WHO Country Representative for Guyana, based in Georgetown, Guyana.

September 1973 – July 1977
Chief of Planning and Evaluation, Health, and Population Division of the Regional Office, PAHO/WHO, covering the Region of the Americas, based in Washington D.C., USA.

September 1977, 3 months
Served as a special representative of the Director of PAHO/WHO and carried out a Study of the PAHO/WHO technical cooperation in the Caribbean.

!978 – 1980
PAHO/WHO Representative for the Western Caribbean, including Jamaica, Bahamas, Bermuda, Cayman Islands, Turks and Caicos Islands and Belize, based in Kingston, Jamaica.

1981-1983
Chief of the Division of Comprehensive Health Services in PAHO/WHO Regional Office, Washington D.C.

!983-1985
Deputy Director of the Office of Health-For-All Strategy Coordination, WHO, Headquarters, Geneva.

1985 – 1989
Director of the Health-For-All Strategy Coordination and Evaluation Office, WHO Headquarters, Geneva.

1989-1993
WHO Representative in Indonesia and WHO Liaison Officer for the Non-Aligned Nations' Health Section, Based in Jakarta, Indonesia1993

Took Early Retirement from WHO in 1993

Zone 1 Advisor in Maternal and Child Health and Population Dynamics 1968-1970

My entry into the World Health Organization was unexpected and unplanned. I think it was a matter of luck and coincidence: being the right person in the right place and supported by the right people.

Trinidad and Tobago needed a medical person for the training of their doctors and nurses in the latest contraceptive technologies. The country had just approved a National Population Policy and wanted to launch a nationwide Family Planning Program. That required setting up family planning services as part of maternal and child health services in the health institutions, including rural health centers. Dr. Max Awon, Minister of Health, requested the services of a consultant from the PAHO Director, Dr. Abraham Horwitz. This person had to be a medical specialist, preferably an OB/Gyn specialist, who could help develop the national program and train the doctors and nurse-midwives in contraceptive technologies. PAHO did not have the budget for this position, so an agreement was reached between PAHO and the Institute for the Study of Human Reproduction, Columbia University (Dr. Wishik was the Director of the Institute and I was serving as a Senior Research Fellow) to send me to PAHO for two years, with a grant that would cover a major part of my salary. I happened to meet all the qualifications required for the work. So, in March 1968, I went off to Port of Spain, Trinidad, with my one suitcase and a carry-on bag. Those were my only possessions at that time.

When my assignment was announced to PAHO Zone 1 Office and PAHO office in Trinidad, the major concern expressed by almost everyone was that I was very young, being the youngest ever medical officer appointed by WHO. But the Ministry of Health had already accepted my assignment. They were more concerned about having someone with the qualification needed for the job, than the age or nationality of the person. And Trinidad had a large proportion of its population from India, so the country accepted and welcomed my assignment.

My two-year assignment in Trinidad was very successful, productive, and enjoyable. I very quickly established good working relationships with everyone involved in the Population Policy and National Family Planning Program. I visited many health centers, trained doctors and nurses in Family Planning techniques, and started family planning services, integrating them with maternal and child health services in rural and urban health centers. Together with the health education officer, of the Ministry of

Health, we developed guides for sex education in schools. With the Population Council of Trinidad and Tobago, we continued to refine the Population Policy, bringing in different sectors: Health, Social Services, Education, and community development. We also improved the collaboration of three major agencies involved in implementing the National Population Policy, including the Ministry of Health, Planned Parenthood Agency, and Catholic Marriage Advisory Council. I was also discovered a Trinidadian medical person, who was working in Guyana, and encouraged her to go to the USA for a Master of Public Health (MPH) degree, with a major in Maternal and Child Health and Family Planning, at the University of Michigan, on a PAHO Scholarship. She completed her studies and returned to Trinidad during the second year of my stay. She was appointed as Medical Officer in the Ministry of Health, in charge of Family Planning Program.

During the second year of my assignment, I was also requested to provide technical assistance, especially training health workers in family planning techniques and developing communication education programs in family planning. These included Guyana, Dominica, St. Kitts-Nevis, and St. Lucia. Barbados and Jamaica already had developed their national Family Planning Programs and were implementing services in their health centers.

At this time, the United Nations Development Program (UNDP) also wanted to start technical projects in Population Dynamics/Family Planning, serving Latin America and the Caribbean. To explore the needs, UNDP assembled a Fact-Finding Mission to review training needs and facilities for Population Dynamics/Family Planning in Mexico, Costa Rica, and Jamaica. UNDP requested my services for this from PAHO and Dr. Horwitz agreed to send me. The Mission reviewed the existing education institutions in Public Health in these three countries and developed a proposal for UNDP for establishing a training program in Family Planning for Latin America in the School of Public Health, Mexico.

The World Bank, under the leadership of Robert McNamara, also wanted the Bank to review the possibility of starting a program on Health and Population. It set up an Interagency Mission for a Feasibility Study to explore the possibility of setting up this program. The Mission was asked to explore the feasibility of starting a World Bank funded Population project in Jamaica. The Bank requested PAHO/WHO to send me to this Mission. (It is important to mention that at this time, I was one of the very few professionals fully trained in the latest techniques of Family Planning, as well as having direct experience in the field in setting up programs and training activities.)

My technical expertise and contribution to the countries in starting their Family Planning Programs and Population Dynamics was recognized in the Region and in the International Arena. There were very few, if any, physicians with expertise: clinical and administrative. Working in the real arena of countries exploring these new and sometimes controversial cultural and politically challenging policies and programs, gave me a unique opportunity to expand my knowledge and skills in developing policies, understanding the politics of health and development, and forming effective collaborative approaches between different agencies. One interesting example was the role of the Catholic Church in collaborating with the National Population Policy Programs. They created a Catholic Marriage Advisory Program to teach and support the practice of restraint and caution in reproductive health. This program promoted the Rhythm method and taught the need to use hormone pills to nurture regular menstrual periods, essential for the method's success.

The information about my skills and expertise led both the World Bank and the UNDP to seek my services on a permanent basis in starting their respective new Programs in Population and Health.

Yet Another Turn Of My Life's Journey

Breaking the Glass Ceiling

Both the World Bank and UNDP were impressed by my work in their first-ever missions to countries exploring their own future involvement in Population Control/Family Planning Programs.

The World Bank decided to establish a Health and Population Division in its Washington Headquarter Office and appointed Dr. K. Kanagaratnam, Chief of the World Bank Jamaica Mission, as Director. Dr. Kanagaratnam invited me to join this Division as the Director of Training. I asked for a month to think about the implication of this on my future professional direction.

In the meantime, UNDP invited me to its Office in New York to meet with Dr. Sankar Menon, head of its Population and Development Office. He asked me if I would consider joining his office to spearhead the Population Program. This was the precursor of the United Nations Fund for Population Activities (UNFPA), a UN Agency established under the UNDP a couple of years later. If I had accepted this offer, I would most probably have been appointed Head of this Agency. Yet, my response to Sankar Menon," No, not all the money in the world or any position would incite me to live in New York." That was the end of that story.

In the meantime, somehow Dr. Horwitz became aware of these offers. My two-year assignment in Trinidad was ending. I was expecting to either return to Columbia University to continue my assignment at the Institute of Human Reproduction and the Medical School or join the World Bank. Dr. Wishik encouraged me to stay in the international field, as he felt that I could make a good contribution with my knowledge and skills and help the Developing countries in their health and family planning programs.

Dr. Horwitz invited me to his office in Washington D.C. to discuss my future. He told me that he was interested in my continuing to work in PAHO/WHO, as the Organization needed more professionals like me. He told me that both the Governments of Guyana and Jamaica had requested my technical expertise in their health programs. He also invited me to consider any relevant position in PAHO/Washington Office. I wasn't keen on moving to the PAHO HQ. office as I preferred to work in the country field offices. During my work in the Caribbean, I had the opportunity of working in Guyana, helping to formulate their National Maternal Health Policy and Program. The Minister of Health, Dr. Sylvia Talbot, was a professional Health Educator and a very active and energetic woman. She liked my work and wanted me to move to Guyana.

Guyana had recently obtained her independence from the United Kingdom (1966) and was in the early stages of establishing National Policies and Programs under the strong leadership of its newly elected President, Mr. Forbes Burnham. UNDP had just opened its new office in Georgetown, the capital of Guyana. PAHO was assisting in the Malaria Control Program through a small team of consultants, including a medical officer and a technical officer. PAHO was considering starting a country office, because the Ministry of Health was requesting more technical assistance, especially in Nursing Education, National Health Policy Development, education of Rural Health workers, Health Education, and Water Supply and Sanitation programs. The position of the Country Representative for PAHO Office was open. I told Dr. Horwitz that I might consider this position.

Dr. Horwitz was surprised and shocked at my request. His response was: *"WHO has never appointed a woman as a Country Representative (Head of its Country Office).*

I responded to him: "*But that is not my problem. You had asked me what job in PAHO would interest me. As I have worked in Guyana, I feel I can make a good contribution there, especially with the current Minister of Health and her staff.*" Dr. Horowitz asked me to wait a while before making any decision, as he would have to consult with Dr. Candau, the Director General of WHO. I returned to Trinidad to continue my assignment.

I was later told that Dr. Candau did not agree to appointing a woman as PAHO/WHO Country Representative. "*Over my dead body!*" apparently, he said.

Since I didn't hear anything from the PAHO Office for a month, I decided to accept the World Bank offer and sent my letter of resignation to the PAHO Zone 1 Office. Dr. Alfred Gerald, the Chief of Zone 1, called Dr. Horwitz about that. Dr. Horwitz then told him to go ahead and offer me the post of PAHO/WHO Country Representative in Guyana, without my knowing.

I was conducting a training workshop for nurses in Nevis (an island of St. Kitts-Nevis), when I received a call from the Minister of Health of St. Kitts-Nevis, congratulating me on my appointment as PAHO/WHO Country Representative in Guyana. He had received a telegram from the Zone 1 Chief, Dr. Gerald, who wanted to talk to me immediately. I called him from Nevis. He told me that he had received my letter of resignation at the same time as a call from Dr. Horwitz about my appointment. Dr. Horwitz of course emphasized to him that I would be the first woman appointed as a PAHO/WHO Country Representative and that if I turned it down, it would be bad for women in the future, especially as Dr. Horwitz had made a special effort for my assignment with the WHO Director General.

This of course put me in a dilemma, yet I knew that my heart was in the work with countries especially Guyana and not with the World Bank which to me sounded very bureaucratic and far from the people. Besides I didn't like the idea of moving to Washington D.C. I preferred to live in the field, closer to people and communities that could be helped. I accepted PAHO's offer and declined the World Bank's offer.

WHO's First Female Country Representative in the World

I moved to Guyana in 1970 and had the most satisfying 3-year assignment there. Whenever people ask me which country and assignment in my work with WHO was the best for me, I always think of Guyana. It was a newly independent country with strong leadership: Hon. Forbes Burnham as its Prime Minister, as well as many other capable and progressive-thinking leaders in politics, government, and community. There was a palpable enthusiasm to move the country forward, developing its first Five-Year Development Plan.

PAHO had a small office within the Ministry of Health and a few technical/professional/administrative staff. The Minister of Health, Dr. Sylvia Talbot, was a Health Educator with a PhD in Public Health/Health Education. She had a team of dedicated professional and administrative staff. Some names that come to my mind are Dr. Robert Baird (Chief Medical Officer); Dr. Alwyn Egbert (Principal Medical Officer, Public Health); Dr. Marchant (Principal Medical Officer, Medical Care); Ms. Gloria Noel (Principal Nursing Officer) etc.

During my three-year assignment in Guyana, PAHO was actively assisting the Ministry of Health in developing its First Five-Year Health Plan. Among the major projects were Malaria Control, Nursing Education, Education of Rural Health Care Auxiliary workers, Strengthening of Rural Health Services, Water Supply, and Sanitation Services. In fact, for the latter, PAHO was able to get funding from UNDP for a feasibility study in Georgetown and the neighboring counties. It is through that project that I met *Steven G. Serdahely*, PAHO Regional Advisor in Water Supply and Sanitation, in the Washington D.C. Regional Office. He was supervising the project. On our first meeting in my office for this project, we felt an immediate soul connection that developed into a long-lasting friendship. We married 14 years later in Geneva. Guyana therefore has even a more special meaning in my life's journey.

NOTE:

(In 2016, Guyana celebrated the 50th Anniversary of its independence from Great Britain. I was invited by the Government to participate in this ceremony as its special guest and was recognized with a special award for being the first PAHO Country Representative and for my contribution to the development of National Health Plan and its health services during those early years of the independence. I felt deeply honored. I was invited to speak at this occasion and to dinner with both the President and the Prime Minister. It was a memorable trip, another opportunity to visit one of my favorite countries in the world. Georgetown still seems the same, with its beautiful homes on stilts, its many gates, and canals to keep the water out, as it is below the sea level.)

Onward To My Next Professional Assignment

I was approached by the Director of PAHO, Dr. Horwitz, to move to its HQ, in Washington D.C., as Chief of Programming and Evaluation Unit of the Health and Population Dynamic Division, whose director was Dr. Richard Prindle. I moved to Washington D.C. in 1972.

PAHO at this time was actively involved in Latin America, assisting countries to develop Population Policies, National Family

Planning Programs, and the training of Health and Community Development workers in Family Planning and Community Education. Funding support for the countries for these programs came from many sources, including US AID, UNDP, World Bank, and some European countries (Germany and Nordic Countries).

My major role was to support countries in formulating their National Programs: plans for training of their health and community development personnel and the evaluation of their Family Planning Programs and Projects. Major projects were in Mexico, Colombia, and Chile, with some activities beginning in other countries. Family Planning was still in its early stages in most Latin American countries (the majority being Catholic). It was being introduced mainly as a component of maternal health services.

In my four-year assignment in this program, I became fluent in Spanish and visited practically all countries in the Region. It was a very busy assignment, not always as satisfying as a country assignment, where one feels that one can have more impact of one's work; there is some continuity of engagement. Perhaps the most memorable work during this phase was in Mexico, Colombia, and the Caribbean.

During one of the country program evaluation meetings in St. Kitts, I met The UNFPA Representative assigned to the Caribbean, Dr. Dieter Ehrhardt. We were monitoring a UNFPA funded small Family Planning project in St. Kitts-Nevis. Dieter was based in the UNFPA Caribbean office in Kingston, Jamaica. I, at this phase of my life, was trying to distance myself from my relationship with Steve. He was married and I didn't want our friendship to evolve into a relationship that would cause break-up of his marriage, even though he admitted that his marriage was not going to continue. He was just waiting for his son, from that marriage to complete school. Then he would move out of that relationship. Yet, that was not acceptable to me as I didn't want to be a factor in breaking his marriage. It had to be his decision, if ever that happened.

In St. Kitts, followed by a visit to Dominica, Dieter and I felt some mutual attraction and we bonded well. This was later followed by a decision to marry, both of us had never been married. (I was 38 and Dieter was 42.)

In 1974, in PAHO's Regional election, Dr. Hector Acuna was elected as the Director of PAHO. Dr. Horwitz moved out of PAHO. Dr. Acuna wanted to reorganize the PAHO's Field Offices structure and especially wanted to strengthen PAHO Technical cooperation in the Caribbean. By this time, most of the Caribbean countries had become independent of Great Britain and were engaged in strengthening their public services, including public health services.

Dr. Acuna gave me a special assignment, to study PAHO/WHO Co-operation in the Caribbean and make recommendations about its future direction and structure. During the 60's when PAHO's Technical Advisory services were started in the Caribbean, they were coordinated by the PAHO Zone I Office based in Venezuela. During the 60's, many of these countries gained their independence from Great Britain and were actively strengthening their health care services. The demands for technical cooperation from PAHO/WHO and other Aid Agencies was increasing. It was important for PAHO to review its technical cooperation program with the Caribbean.

During 1975-1976, I carried out this assessment and made recommendations about its future direction and structure. I visited every country in the Caribbean and consulted with many officials at policy, managerial, and community levels. Following this assessment, I made recommendations to the Director; one of that was to create a Caribbean Office Coordinator's office, based in Barbados. The Office was to be headed by a person designated as the Caribbean Program Coordinator and supported by several technical advisors who would provide technical support to all the Caribbean countries. This report and its recommendations were presented to the Ministers of Health of the Caribbean countries at a special meeting held in St. Kitts.

Dr. Acuna wanted to appoint me as the Head of this office, but I suggested to him that it would be a better political strategy to appoint a Caribbean person to this office. I didn't think it was wise to appoint someone from outside the Caribbean. Besides, I didn't want this job. At this time, I had other plans. Dieter Ehrhardt, UNFPA Coordinator based in Kingston, Jamaica asked me to marry him, and I agreed. That also meant that I wanted to be stationed in Jamaica and wanted to be PAHO/WHO Country Representative in Jamaica. This was in fact a sub-regional office in the Caribbean that covered Jamaica, Bahamas, Bermuda, Turks and Caicos Islands, Cayman Islands and Belize. Dr. Acuna agreed to my request. On June 24,1977, Dieter and I got married at my home in Virginia with just a few friends in attendance.

In August 1977, I was transferred to Kingston, Jamaica, as PAHO/WHO Representative to Jamaica, Bahamas, Bermuda, Belize, Cayman Islands, and Turks and Caicos Islands. It was a very engaging job, requiring travel to all these countries, for planning health services, developing training programs for health workers, developing water supply and sanitation services, Nursing Education, Veterinary Public Health Services, etc. It was a large office with several professional/technical and administrative staff.

Regretfully our marriage didn't work well as within the first three months of our marriage, I realized that it was a mistake. Both of us had never been married before and at ages 38 and 42, it is difficult to change one's values and habits too much. Dieter's expectation from the marriage were quite different from mine. He expected me to be home by 5 pm and spend more time with him playing, etc. For me, my work has always been first and foremost, and the demands of this large office were high. I wasn't prepared to give that a second priority. We both didn't want children anyway.

After the first year of our marriage, Dieter was transferred to Nairobi, Kenya. Prior to that, we were able to take a trip to Germany to meet his family: mother and sister, and her family. Dieter's mother, *Mutti*, was in her 80's, a strong, tall, and beautiful woman, very down to earth, who had seen two wars, lost her husband early, and brought up her two children by herself. I really liked her. We also visited India and met my mummy, Behanji, and her family. Mummy liked Dieter. Her comment, "I am glad you married an Aryan", surprised me, as did her acceptance of Dieter and my marrying a non-Indian. Shows - one never fully knows one's parents well.

Dieter left for Nairobi in 1978 and we knew that our marriage was over. It was just a question of time and convenience when the divorce would officially take place. In the meantime, I continued to enjoy my work with its very enthusiastic people and very dedicated staff. The work involved a lot of travel, both within Jamaica and to other islands. I made some great friendships during this time, many of them have lasted my lifetime.

During this period, Dr. Halfdan Mahler, the Director General of WHO, visited Jamaica on an official visit. WHO's World Health Assembly had just approved its Goal of Health-For-All by the Year 2000, and WHO was now looking for models in countries that were implementing this. Jamaica was well advanced in developing its Primary Health Care Strategy and Services, and Dr. Mahler wanted to see this firsthand. His visit was memorable. It engaged many high-level officials, including the Prime Minister. Dr. Mahler was very impressed by the work we were doing and especially the involvement of PAHO/WHO. Dr. Acuna, PAHO Director, also accompanied him on this visit and felt very proud and protective of me. I feel that he might have detected Dr. Mahler's interest in me as a potential staff in WHO HQ.

An Unexpected Move In My Professional Journey – Again

Dr. Mahler, Director General of WHO showed an interest in my coming to WHO HQ., Geneva to a position in his office as Health-For-All Strategy Coordinator. I feel that somehow Dr. Acuna, Director of PAHO, got news of this. He sent Dr. Paul Ehrlich, the Deputy Director of PAHO to Jamaica, to talk to me about moving to PAHO in Washington D.C. as Chief of the Division of Comprehensive Health Services. The Chief of this Division, Dr. Develiers had resigned. The Division was the biggest Program Division with 120 staff positions in PAHO/WHO Regional Office and in the field. The Division was responsible for many major PAHO programs, including Health Policy, Health Planning, Maternal and Child Health, Nutrition, and Health Information Systems. The Division had weak leadership over the past 3 years and many positions, both in the HQ. as well as in the field, were vacant.

I must say, I was very surprised at this news. I was going to India on my home leave soon, so I agreed to pass through Washington to meet with the Director. When I met him, he asked me to take this post, Chief of the Division of Comprehensive Health Services. I asked Dr. Acuna if this might be a political risk for him, as it was one of the most prominent and prestigious position in PAHO. I was not even from any country of this Region, let alone being a woman. There had never been a woman Chief of a Division of a Regional Office. How would this look to the countries of the Region? Will they accept me as Chief of a major Division in PAHO.?

Dr. Acuna's response was, "The Division is very crucial to the success of PAHO's Programs in the Region. It is in a mess, and I feel that you are the most qualified to organize and make it effective. As far as any political risk is concerned, I am willing to take that and if the leaders in the countries disagree with my decision, they can remove me at the next election."

I felt very honored. I agreed to consider this offer and give my response soon. On my way to India for my home leave, I passed through Geneva and met with Dr. Mahler, during the World Health Assembly. He asked me to consider moving to WHO/HQ in Geneva. It was not clear to me what my function would be. And in fact, I felt a bit of hostility, and may be jealousy, from some of the senior staff in the Director General's Office. So, I didn't give a definitive response. I just said that I would consider it. (Although, at this time I had already decided that I would not move to WHO/HQ. It seemed to me too vague, confusing, and a very political environment).

Coincidentally, during this visit, the Prime Minister of India, Mrs. Indira Gandhi, was in Geneva and addressed the World Health Assembly. I had the opportunity of meeting her. It was a great experience, but I also felt that Indians in WHO/HQ at this time felt very suspicious and even jealous about my being there, seated between her and the Director General. Dr. Mahler introduced me to her with very positive comments about me.

I also visited Nairobi to see Dieter and he agreed to take the necessary steps to dissolve our marriage as mutual consent.

While in Delhi, I informed the PAHO Director that I would accept the post of the Director of the Division of Comprehensive Health Services. Within 24 hours, I received a telegram from PAHO, congratulating me on my appointment. This had been kept a secret until all sides had agreed as the Director did not want any political turmoil.

BREAKING THE GLASS CEILING AGAIN - THE FIRST WOMAN APPOINTED AS CHIEF OF A DIVISION IN A REGIONAL OFFICE OF WHO AND PAHO

I received a fond farewell from Jamaican authorities and moved to Washington D.C., in August 1980, to take up my position as the Chief of the Division of Comprehensive Health Services. I bought a beautiful house in Lake Barcroft, Falls Church, Virginia and moved there.

(An interesting anecdote: Two persons from the moving company who had moved me from Guyana to Washington D.C. and then from Washington D.C. to Jamaica and again moved and unpacked my household stuff when I moved back to Washington D.C. after Jamaica remarked, "You again".)

Chief of the Division of Comprehensive Health Services, PAHO/WHO
1980-1983

Comprehensive Health Services Division was the largest Division in PAHO. I had 112 professional/technical and administrative staff working under my supervision in the Regional Office and many more in country offices. I had responsibility over four sub-regional offices including: Caribbean Food and Nutrition Center in Jamaica; Institute of Nutrition in Central America in Guatemala; Center for Health Planning in Chile; and Center for Perinatology and Maternal and Child Health in Uruguay. The Division's Budget was $60 million.

It was an incredible responsibility given to me and I was only 41 years old, the first woman appointed as a Head of a Division in PAHO. My first task was to fill the vacant positions - more than a third of the posts were vacant when I took over.

It was a very demanding post, perhaps the most intense and demanding that I had ever had before (or even after). Besides providing policy, technical, and administrative leadership for the Division, I had an extensive travel schedule. This required visiting many countries of Latin America, for project reviews, supervision, and attending official meetings of the Governments. For one year, sometimes I had to travel more than 100 days. But I was single (again), with no personal responsibilities at home, and could travel freely. My beautiful house in Falls Church, Virginia, near Lake Barcroft, had a 1/3rd acre of land around it and lots of oak trees. I made many new friends, and many members of my family visited me in this beautiful home. I hosted several parties with PAHO staff, visiting dignitaries, and friends and family.

But it was a grueling and demanding job- most days I spent more than 12 hours in the office and 40-45 minutes of travel from home to office and return each way.

As I look back at my major accomplishments during this period, a few stand out.

Number one was recruiting several women professionals in my Division and in PAHO in general. There had always been a resistance to recruiting women in professional positions in WHO. I recall when selecting a woman for the post of Regional Health Education Advisor, I was told that she did not have enough international experience for the post. My comment was, "How can she have experience unless she gets an opportunity to be in an international environment?" Besides, there were two other factors against her recruitment: she was black and a woman. But I insisted and she went on to be a successful professional. Later, she was appointed as a PAHO/WHO Country Representative.

During the first year of my appointment as Division Chief, I filled all vacancies in the Division and completed reorganization of the Division. And during my tenure of three years, I visited every county in the Latin American Region and took the opportunity to see clinics and rural health services firsthand. I met with local Government officials, Ministers of Health, other top-level Government officials, and even Presidents. I was in Santiago, Chile, when President Allende was ousted. I was in Buenos Aires, Argentina, when a coup toppled the President of that country. I was at an official party and suddenly saw the army marching in the streets. We were told there was a coup – a peaceful one - and the party continued. We were eventually escorted to our hotels with army guards. I gave an official lecture in Spanish to the Mexican Academy of Science on "Health of The Americas". I represented WHO in the International Conference on Women in Mexico and gave my speech in Spanish on behalf of WHO. That surprised and confused my Caribbean colleagues, as they were expecting me to speak in English. I also facilitated the meeting of the Ministers of Health of the Caribbean on Primary Health Care and so on.

During this period of life, I developed fluency in Spanish and learnt about the political history of Latin America. The Region was going through a political awakening, with many countries aided by USAID moving to the Left. This was challenged by the existing and suppressive regimes, leading to the murder of Allende in Chile, the isolation of Cuba, and unrest in many Central American countries, also leaning to the Left. One of the most affected was Nicaragua, which had been ruled by an autocratic and suppressive dictator, Somoza, who was mainly interested in advancing his business enterprises. His suppression of the masses eventually led to a revolution, under the leadership of Manuel Ortega. The United States helped to evacuate Somoza and his cronies to Florida, where he spent the rest of his life. Nicaragua and Cuba became close partners. Cuba helped Nicaragua in developing the policies of the new regime toward the Left, under the leadership of Ortega.

I visited both Cuba and Nicaragua during this period. The Government of Cuba wanted WHO to review its Primary Health Care system, and only wanted me to do this. I guess my not being linked politically to any of the Latin American countries and being an Indian citizen (Cuba had a good relationship with India as a member of the non-aligned movement), Cuban leaders trusted me to make an objective and impartial review. During this visit, I met President Fidel Castro and found him a dynamic speaker. I also had a refreshing experience of visiting a health care system that was well managed and provided good quality health care to all its citizens. My report and recommendations were well received by senior health officials.

Nicaragua moved ahead with its socialist policies. I was invited by its government, along with the Regional Chief of UNICEF office, to be present at a ceremony celebrating the 5th Anniversary of the establishment of its National Health System. It was a memorable visit, During the ceremony held outside in the open square of the City of Managua, Manuel Ortega spoke for more than two hours, under a torrential rain. Everyone was totally drenched, but not one person dared to move. The entire diplomatic community was there, sitting in that rain, listening to the Patriotic speech of Ortega. No one dared open an umbrella. These were covering only the sound equipment. The rest of the speeches were short and then the Ceremony was followed by a parade in the streets. At this time, I and my UNICEF colleague managed to escape to our hotel, that was on the way, to get out of the rain, change our soaking clothes, and rest and warm up with a shot of rum before we went to the evening reception.

There were many such exciting moments, especially during my visits to the countries. However, the work in PAHO-Washington office was very demanding. Much of it was managing the staff and budget, and of course attending numerous official meetings. I was accepted by the staff as being the Chief of the Division and hence their supervisor/boss, however, I was also aware that some of the senior staff in the Division, especially from Latin American countries, who were mostly men, deep inside resented being under a younger woman, not even from this Region. I utilized my diplomatic skills, patience, as well as my personal inner strength, to deal with this challenge and earn their respect. But it was exhausting. I worked almost 12 hours a day, often even during the weekends. I used to set aside one Sunday in a month, when I wouldn't speak to anyone, and spend a quiet reflective time in my beautiful, serene home. This helped me to recover my strength and poise. No doubt, the stress was also taking a toll on my health. I began to note occasional higher blood pressure. I joined a gym where I would go after work.

In 1983, PAHO had its election of the Director. There was an intense political campaign against the current Director, Dr. Acuna. Several senior staff within PAHO were actively promoting Dr. Carlyle Guerra de Macedo from Brazil. I refused to participate in any political activity. I was a professional civil servant in the United Nations and remained neutral, even though I was being asked to influence the Caribbean vote since I was well known and respected by the Caribbean countries. I also felt that if Dr. Macedo won the election, there would be a major reorganization of PAHO, something that usually happens after the elections. A new leader brings his/her own vision to the Organization, that usually results in changes both in the structure and the people within the system. I was also aware that during any 'reorganization' process, a lot of energy, at least initially, goes into infighting, with senior staff jockeying for positions etc. Not much real work gets done. I felt that perhaps it was time for me to move.

Dr. Halfdan Mahler, the Director-General of WHO also attended the PAHO Regional Assembly, as was customary during the PAHO Director's election year. Before the election, we had a talk and he asked me to come to the Geneva HQ Office of WHO. I tentatively agreed and requested him to let Dr. Macedo know once he was elected, as I didn't want my decision to be linked to his election. I was quite sure that he would win the election. I really liked him and was pretty sure that he would provide a fresh new Vision to PAHO. (Some Caribbean countries had earlier even approached me to run for the election, but I refused as I didn't want to be a part of any political process.)

When Dr. Macedo was elected as the next Director of PAHO, in May 1983, I decided to move to WHO HQ in Geneva, as Deputy to the Director of Health-for-All Strategy Coordination Office, under the Director General's Office. Dr. Joshua Cohen, special Policy Advisor to the Director General, worked out a deal. The post was a P5 level, but since I was already at P6/D1 level, he suggested that I be moved to the existing P5 level. I refused. I noted that Personnel rules allow me to keep my current grade level, even if I moved to a lower grade, but that was not acceptable to me. The position itself needed to be upgraded. He had to agree. Another political/bureaucratic maneuver that shows it is important to learn the rules and persist. Never let the system dictate your position.

A MAJOR PROFESSIONAL AND PERSONAL MOVE
ONWARD TO WHO HQ, GENEVA –
BEGINNING OF A NEW DIRECTION OF MY CAREER

After completing fifteen years (1969-1983) with PAHO, I gave a fond farewell, sold my beautiful house in Virginia, and moved to WHO Headquarters, Geneva, as Deputy Director of the Office of Health-For-All Strategy Coordination, under the Director General's Office. Dr. Hakan Hellberg, a very gentle and likable person from Finland, was the Director. He had recently joined WHO after a career with several not-for-profit organizations, mainly in Africa. My responsibility was primarily the monitoring and evaluation of the implementation of Health-For-All Strategy and following up with countries regarding their policies and programs to achieve the Goal of Health-For-All by the year 2,000, as approved by the World Health Assembly.

The World Health Assembly, in 1978, had approved a Landmark Resolution: *Achieving the Goal of Health-For-All by the Year 2000, defining 12 health indicators that must be aimed for by each country.* Realizing that this was an ambitious goal, the World Health Assembly had agreed to monitor the progress every two years and evaluate every four years. My responsibility was to coordinate this effort.

Even though I had 15 years of experience in PAHO/WHO, I was new to the politics and bureaucracy of WHO-HQ. My previous experience and work were not well known, or even recognized, in this new environment. I had not come to the WHO HQ from the usual rank and file. I had not been recommended by any Government. I had no political connection, nor was I subservient to anyone. I had come with my professional and technical credentials. I realized soon, that wasn't enough in this new environment. In WHO HQ, it was a different game altogether. Many senior positions were filled by politically endorsed persons, representing, proportionately, WHO's different regions. Even though I was originally from India and still had Indian citizenship, the Indian Government had not recommended me, nor did they even know about me. Since I was not a citizen of any of the countries of the American Region, I was not endorsed by any, even though they knew about me and my work in that Region. Many WHO HQ staff viewed me as someone different, not known to them. Some regarded me with suspicion, some with jealousy, as I was close to the Director-General and had access to him when I needed. Besides, I was a woman, the only one at that time in WHO HQ at grade D1. There was one woman professional, Director of a Division, at D2 level.

My post was new and so were its functions. My first task was to produce the First Monitoring Report of the implementation of WHO's Strategy for Health-For-All. I moved to WHO HQ in September 1983 and the First Report was to be presented to the WHO Executive Board in January 1984. I had just three months to prepare. 119 countries had submitted their reports. My challenge was to distill from these the essence/information that showed some progress. In fact, the country reports were very general. I had to literally extract information that could be presented to the Executive Board. Fortunately, I had good help in preparing the presentation in a graphic form, using computer technology that was in its early stages. It was the first time this type of presentation was given in WHO. Several senior staff were concerned, even skeptical, as first, they didn't know me well, second, I was just newly assigned to WHO HQ, and third, I was a woman from a Third World country. Fortunately, I had good help from a junior staff statistician from the Division of Health Information Systems.

The presentation went very well, appreciated by the members of the Board. That also made several senior staff jealous of me, maybe they felt threatened. This was my first experience to witness political jockeying in WHO HQ, especially among men, but even from the women in senior positions. It presented me a good learning experience in international politics, in WHO HQ. I became very watchful about this during the rest of my stay in WHO HQ. There was more to come.

The Director-General was pleased with my performance, and he changed the title of my job to Deputy Director of the HFA Strategy Coordination Office. That led to even more jealousy among the senior staff. Within 2 years of my assignment, Dr. Hellberg had moved to another Division within the HQ and I was elevated to the post of the Director of HFA Strategy Coordination Office, the highest level (D-2) that one can reach in the UN system without being in a political position, such as the Assistant Director-General or Deputy Director-General. Several senior staff in the HQ began to project me as potentially the next Director-General of WHO to succeed once Dr. Mahler decided to retire. But this story will come later.

My next major challenge was to develop Leadership for Health-for-All, a new global Initiative that the Director General announced to the World Health Assembly. When I asked him who will take on this challenge, he replied, "YOU". That came as a surprise and presented a huge challenge for me. No one had undertaken Leadership Development, especially in the public sector. A few books were available that dealt mainly with prominent individuals who had demonstrated success, financial/managerial in the private sector, or some political leaders.

Over the next four years, I studied a lot about leadership and made a worldwide enquiry about the values, characteristics etc. of leaders in public/social/education/community sectors. I put together a team of like-minded individuals from WHO/HQ and from public health educational institutions that had demonstrated leadership, taking their institutions into a more creative path. During this period, my team conducted Leadership Development Colloquia/Training programs in all Regions of WHO, and colloquia for top leaders from Public/Education/Community sectors of many countries of the world. These were held in the Island of Brioni, Yugoslavia, a venue offered by the Government of Yugoslavia.

Brioni happened to be the place where the Non-Aligned Treaty was signed by Nehru, Nasser, and Tito, three great leaders of India, Egypt, and Yugoslavia. It was a historic event and Brioni island was preserved by the Government of Yugoslavia as a special historic place. The island was used only for special historic events, and we were fortunate to have been offered this place *free* by the Government of Yugoslavia for HFA Leadership Development. This was a very special privilege. One had to go to Brioni via a ferry and once our participants were there, there was no escape for them. They had to engage in dialogues.

The four years of my work in Leadership Development for Health-for-All was probably the most challenging and satisfying work for me. I got to know many 'leaders', from many countries of the world. I developed a new form of communication, a conversation rather than the usual kind of teaching or discussion. These were dialogues without judgement, with deep listening, and open to many ways of providing leadership. Through these dialogues, I learnt about humility, acceptance of different points of view, cultural characteristics of leadership, etc.

There was no doubt that this experience changed me. I believe I became more connected to my own values and ethics and felt more in charge of my destiny. So, when the change of the Director-

General came in 1988, through a politically manipulated process (my feeling was that the WHO Leadership Position had been bought), I decided that I couldn't work under that leadership. No doubt having worked in Leadership Development for HFA, I had become well-known in the world of Public Health. Several senior people from many countries even encouraged me to go for the position of Director-General. But I knew that, as I was still a Citizen of India, I would have to be recommended by the Government of India. I would have to play a larger political role and I just couldn't see myself doing that. I was not that ambitious, and I didn't want to compromise my values for a position.

The position of the Director-General of WHO had become more politically driven. Not surprisingly, as many newly independent countries in Africa and Asia were learning the value of their partnership in the International Community. They wanted their voices to be heard and respected. The International Development Field, until 1980, was dominated by the Anglo-Western world and by men. Practically all UN Organizations were headed by men (mostly white men). After the World Conference on Equality for Women in the early eighties, some token women were appointed in higher positions in the U.N. Organizations.

Personal Note:

In the early eighties, I also reconnected with my friend, Steven Serdahely. We had remained friends since we first met in Guyana. He was divorced and now feeling free to make a commitment. He took early retirement from his position at the World Bank to be with me. We decided to get married and in 1985, we married in Geneva, in a very simple ceremony. For me, this partnership made my stay in Geneva very enjoyable. We knew that we were soulmates and now joined together for life.

Not wanting to play a political role, I decided to either leave WHO, or move to a country position, preferably as WHO Country

Representative in a large country, such as China or Indonesia. I confronted the Director-General, Dr. Mahler, the day after the election of the new Director-General, and told him that I felt that WHO had been bought out by the Government of Japan (there were rumors that votes of several African and Asian countries had been bought by Japan), and that I don't come with it. I was ready to leave the Organization. He insisted that I stay, as I had much to offer to the countries. I then asked for the post of WHO Country Representative in Indonesia. This was accepted, even over the objection of some of the senior people in the South-East Asia Region, especially the WHO Regional Director. Some felt threatened by my expertise and reputation and even suggested that the Government of Indonesia may not accept a woman to lead their WHO Country Office. This proved to be quite false, as the Minister of Health of Indonesia was very pleased at my appointment. I had been involved in their Leadership Development Program and got to know many of their senior health and university people.

In 1989, after 5 1/2 years of my assignment in WHO/HQ, Geneva, I moved to Indonesia as WHO Country Representative. In view of my senior grade, I was given additional responsibilities, including the WHO Liaison Officer for the Non-Aligned Countries in health development. Indonesia, at this time, had taken on the leadership of the Non-Aligned Countries, so it was appropriate for me to be the focal point for WHO. I was also a liaison officer for the Asia-Pacific Consortium of Public Health Education programs of the Universities and continued my work with them on their leadership development programs.

During my assignment in WHO/HQ, 1983-1989, I had several memorable and unique experiences through my extensive travel schedule, related to the review of Primary Health Care Policy and Strategy development in a number of countries. I was also responsible for the selection of the prestigious Sasakawa (a wealthy Japanese Donor) Health Prize to individuals who had shown special leadership in developing primary health care services, especially in low-income and rural communities. This gave me opportunity to travel to Japan, Burma (Myanmar), India, Mongolia, and China. I visited remote and impoverished areas of these countries and met dedicated leaders who were engaged in bringing health awareness and basic primary care health services to their communities, with their active engagement. I also had the opportunity of visiting Jaipur, India, to see their innovative example of creating "Jaipur-foot", for those individuals who had suffered leg amputations due to a variety of reasons.

All these experiences gave me the unique opportunity to witness the creative and courageous leadership, especially in impoverished areas, of some dedicated leaders. That brought me humility and encouraged me to continue to dedicate my life to serving those who needed more and not to be concerned about my official position and personal concerns - and not to engage in the false ego-building political process. I resolved to continue working in WHO, as long as I could truthfully serve the people. I helped the people to advance and improve the health of their communities, especially the underserved and neglected ones, and to build leadership in health development among the communities, with officials managing health services and educators of health professionals. I also learned Bahasa Indonesia, to be able to converse with the health officials and community leaders.

Sumedha Khanna conducting leadership training of Latin American Public Health Administrators.

Sumedha Khanna developing Health-for-All leadership for Caribbean Ministers of Health.

In Beijing, China
At the HFA-Leadership Colloquium.
(Minister of Health and The Vice chancellor
of Beijing University Besiding)

Sumedha Khanna and the Health-for All Leadership Training Program in China.

Sumedha M Khanna leading the Health Leadership Training Beijing, China, with the Health Minister attending.

Sumedha Khanna World Health Organization Deputy Director of the Office of Health-For-All Strategy Coordination with Southeast Asia Representatives and the WHO Regional Director.

My assignment in WHO/HQ gave me the unique opportunity to:

1. Review the development and progress (or lack of it) of Primary (or at least basic) Health Care Services in countries of Asia and Africa (I was already familiar with the situation in Latin American countries). Among the most notable ones in Africa were Tanzania, Kenya, Zimbabwe, Mozambique and Seychelles) and in Asia the Philippines, Indonesia, Thailand, Nepal and Burma (Myanmar).

2. Study the challenges in the financing of health services. I led a team to review this in several countries and prepared a report for Technical Discussions on this topic at the World Health Assembly. I became aware through these studies, that the financing of health services is a

very complex subject. No country in the world has had full success in achieving this, or in creating an optimum balance in demand, supply, affordability, and access, irrespective of being the most developed, or the least developed.

3. Study and develop Leadership in Health. What are the characteristics of good and effective leaders, if and how leadership can be developed. During a period of four years, I led several colloquia on Leadership development for Health for All, bringing leaders or those in leadership positions, from many countries together, from the health, education, and community development sectors. These were held in Brioni, the island of Croatia that the Government of Yugoslavia dedicated mainly to developing leadership and related events in honor of Nehru, Nasser, and Tito. The Government offered this island to WHO for Health-for-All Leadership Development Colloquia over a period of four years (1984-1988). WHO brought together health and community leaders from over 30 countries from Africa, Asia, and Middle Eastern Regions for these colloquia, facilitated by me, along with colleagues from Yugoslavia and WHO/HQ. I also facilitated inter-country HFA/Leadership Colloquia in the countries of these regions, including in Bangkok for the South-East Asia Region, in Tanzania for the African Region, China for just that country, and in Copenhagen for the European Region. I also organized and facilitated HFA Leadership development Colloquia for Public Health Educational Institutions of the Asia/Pacific Regions.

4. Contact with many top-level leaders, Political, Social, and Community, from many countries of the world, through HFA Leadership activities. Some later became top political leaders in their countries, such as presidents or University Chancellors.

5. Facilitate a specific leadership colloquium for all the Ministers of Health in the Caribbean Region, on Primary Health Care and the role of health and community leaders in developing and advancing the Goal of Health-for-All in their respective countries. This was at a special request from these countries.

6. Facilitate a Technical Discussion at the World Health Assembly in 1988 on Leadership Development for Health-for-All. The year-long preparation for this included a personal letter from me to 150 leaders in health, education, and community development sectors in many countries and educational institutions of the world. I received over 100 responses from this enquiry about "Leadership", a treasure that I have kept with me. I also organized and facilitated the Director-General's Dialogue on Leadership Development for Health-for-All, which included top-level leaders from 25 countries of the world. This was held in Brioni, Yugoslavia. Using the materials that ensued from these discussions and enquiry, I prepared the documents for the Technical Discussions that were attended by over 400 participants. It was a very stimulating event and offered promising advance to the Goal of Health-for-All.

   The Technical Discussions were energized by a Panel that included: Director-General of WHO, Dr. Halfdan Mahler; Dame Nita Barrow, Ambassador of Barbados to the United Nations; Ministers of Health from Argentina, Turkey, Hungary, and Nigeria; University Chancellors/ Heads of Public Health Educational Institutions from the USA, China, and India; and community leaders from Australia and Denmark.

7. Receive the Professor Kazue McLaren Leadership Award, for my work on Leadership Development, especially for the Public Health Educational Institutions in the

Asia-Pacific Regions. This award ceremony was held in Singapore and when the US Ambassador to Singapore called on me to receive the Award, after Professor Dean Michael of the School of Public Health, Hawaii gave comments re my work on leadership development, he exclaimed "Oh! I expected a much older woman."

I can say that after my work in Guyana, I still rank my 25 years of work with WHO as #1. Leadership Development for HFA comes second. This work transformed me and played a major role in my personal and professional development. These two assignments contributed to a major shift in my consciousness and the values about the work that we have the privilege and honor to do in the countries, helping them to advance the health of their people. There is no doubt that the progress is slow, yet the rewards are incalculable.

THEN THE CHANGE HAPPENED -
A NEW DIRECTION IN MY PROFESSIONAL CAREER
Moving back to a Country Assignment.

1988 was the year when Leadership Development for HFA peaked. It was also the year when WHO leadership changed. Despite many requests for the Director-General, D. Halfdan Mahler, to stay on at least for another term, he declined. A hotly contested election ensued. That led to the Japanese Government's actively supporting its candidate, Dr. Hiroshi Nakajima, to be elected as the next Director-General. This was the first time such active and blatant politicization of WHO was felt. WHO Executive Board members from countries in Africa and Asia were, in fact, bribed to cast their vote in favor of Dr. Nakajima. His technical background was more in the field of pharmaceuticals and health technology, rather than public health development.

I anticipated major changes in WHO policies and the future direction of its work, so rather than stay in WHO HQ, I opted to take a WHO Representative assignment in a large country of choice, China, or Indonesia. I was happy to leave the highly politicized WHO/HQ and move to Indonesia, which had WHO's second largest program of Technical Cooperation with 70+ Projects and a large staff. I was also assigned some global responsibilities, including WHO Liaison with the Non-Aligned countries.

A new era began for me. I moved to Jakarta, Indonesia, in 1989 with my life-partner, Steve Serdahely.

Assignment As Who Representative in Indonesia 1989-1993

Working in countries as WHO Technical Consultant or as WHO Country Representative had always been the most gratifying assignment for me. It gave me an opportunity to learn first-hand about the cultural, political, socio-economic development in the general environment and to work closely with the leaders, especially in health, at central, provincial/state and community levels. I witnessed the progress of health development, including the participation of the people. My assignment in Indonesia for five years was one of my most exciting in WHO.

When I asked for a country assignment in China or Indonesia (I couldn't be assigned as a country representative in India, being an Indian citizen), I was told that someone had already been assigned to China. The Regional Director of South-East Asia (SEARO), Dr. U KO KO, expressed some concern about my assignment in Indonesia. He felt that Indonesia might not accept a woman as its WHO Representative, being a predominantly Muslim country, even though it had always presented itself as a secular country. (I believe Dr. U KO KO was threatened by my presence in the SEARO Region). But both the President of Indonesia, Mr. Suharto, and the Minister of Health, Dr. Adhyatma, were delighted and even felt honored that such a senior and experienced person in WHO was being proposed as its Country Representative. It is important to mention that it was rare that a staff member, once assigned to a post in WHO HQ, wished to move to a country assignment. WHO/HQ staff generally felt superior to country staff. They also felt more secure in their jobs, being closer to the political environment, with many of them proposed by their respective governments for these posts. After all, who would want to live in Kenya, Thailand, or Manila after having lived in pristine Geneva, close to all the centers of Europe.

Because of my special and senior position in WHO Hierarchy, I could have asked for any assignment in WHO/HQ, or in the Regional Office of South-East Asia. But I wanted to be in a country as far away as possible from WHO/HQ, closer to people I wanted to serve.

Indonesia is an incredible country, consisting of over 14,000 islands, with a multi-religious population: Hindu (8%); Muslims (90%); and Christians and others (2%). President Suharto was an incredible leader. He saved his country from Chinese invasion and brought up its development status from a very low level to a progressive level, within a period of 20 years. He maintained its secular status, honoring and recognizing all religions. Indonesian women actively participated in the country's development, from village to the central level, under the capable leadership of Mrs. Suharto, the wife of the President.

My five-year assignment in Indonesia gave me an opportunity to get to know its culture and people at all levels. WHO had over 70 projects and the WHO Representative enjoyed an ambassador's status. Indonesia is also a very ceremonious country. Many formal ceremonies were held at the Palace of the President and even at villages presided by the Village Chiefs, during my field visits. I travelled to many of the major islands and learnt firsthand the culture and the status of health activities, while observing WHO project activities. There were so many photographs taken during these visits that I have made them a separate album. I also learned enough Bahasa Indonesia to communicate with people in the villages, especially the health workers.

Among the highlights of my work in Indonesia were:

- A nationwide Safe Motherhood Policy, Strategy and Plan that was accepted by the Government. With almost 80% of Indonesian women giving births at home with trained or untrained local midwives, the maternal death rates were high. Many areas of Indonesia are remote, isolated with little or no transportation. I realized that during my work there, as we often had to travel through many different means.

- A first Nursing Education School in the island of Irian Jaya, one of the remote islands with most inhabitants very primitive ethnic groups. It was a distinct pleasure for me to attend the graduation ceremony of the first graduates of this School. It was fascinating to see the beautifully formally dressed Nursing Graduates celebrating the event surrounded with their scantily clad, primitive families who walked through miles barefoot to attend the ceremony. They brought food, fruits, vegetables, and animals (mostly pigs), which were roasted on the ground, right there. This was a once-in-a-lifetime experience, forever etched in my memory.

- I gave a speech on behalf of WHO at the Non-Aligned Nations' Summit, held in Jakarta, where I met many world leaders and, in fact, was seated next to Yasir Arafat. Another unforgettable experience.

I truly enjoyed my work in Indonesia, where I also had my life-partner Steve Serdahely with me and got my first dog, Lady, a standard dachshund. The years went by so fast. After my three-year assignment was over, I was asked to return to WHO/HQ, as Director of the Family Health Division. I declined and got Government approval to stay in Indonesia for two more years.

In 1993, the election of the Director-General of WHO was scheduled. There were two other candidates preferred by a majority of Latin American and European countries. I was even asked if I would like to be Deputy to one of them if they were elected. My decision was of course to wait and see.

After a bitter election, Dr. Nakajima won the election by one vote. This was unbelievable, so the U.S. Government asked for a roll-call vote at the World Health Assembly, something that had never been done before. But the vote showed that Dr. Nakajima won by winning all votes from Asin, Africa, and many Middle Eastern countries. It was also known that the Government of Japan gave bribes for some of these votes.

The U.S. and European Governments asked the Director-General to set up a special cabinet to oversee the Policy of WHO programs and appoint a strong, unbiased, and capable person to head this cabinet. I was called to the World Health Assembly and the Director-General told me privately that he would like me to lead this special cabinet. I realized that this would be a symbolic position and, if I accepted it, I would be locked in an ineffective position under a politically inspired leadership. I couldn't work under such leadership and compromise my values.

Others might have considered that my decision was not wise, as may be once I took the position, I could change the direction of WHO Policy. I felt otherwise. I had worked in the bureaucracies and governments long enough to know that such a change is not easy, and since it was a bitterly fought election, there would be a lot of infighting that I might get caught in. I felt that I was still young and could move on to something more interesting and worthwhile. After 25 years with WHO, I could take early retirement. (Sometimes I do wonder if this was a good decision, but I would never know now.)

8

Starting An Unknown, Unchartered Journey

1993: Leaving Who After 25 Years Of Service

California - Here we come!

"How does one pursue or hold on to one's values within a bureaucratic system without compromising?"

This was one of the most important challenges of my work in WHO, during my last years. How does one balance between political agenda vs. the professional/service agenda? I felt that once you go into the system from the field/country position to central or regional levels, i.e., from action/Managerial to policy levels, conflict occurs. Policy making inevitably entails politics. And, yes, one must play politics sometimes to get or mobilize resources/funds for programs/projects that can help people. But playing politics for personal gain, in terms of position, is not acceptable to me. Hence my decision to leave WHO rather than accept the Director-General's offer to take the position of his cabinet chief for policy. (I *must admit, there are times I have wondered about this decision, as maybe I could have made a difference – but then, this is history.*)

Being married to Steve, I had already received my Green Card, hence moving to USA was the option that we took. We were first considering returning to Washington D.C./Virginia where

I had lived before, had many friends, and was well known to International Organizations. I even considered the possibility of working as a consultant to the World Bank, or the UNFPA (both these Organizations had contacted me for this possibility). But once we tasted the beautiful climate, sunshine, and warmth of the people, along with the fact that we owned a condo and a townhouse we had purchased earlier, and that my eldest sister and younger brother both lived in Fremont, we decided to settle in Fremont, California.

The question for me was what I was going to do professionally at this phase of my life, at age 55. I wasn't well known in California and did not have any special contacts. I was asked to serve as a consultant by the Western Consortium of Public Health, Berkeley, for a program on Public Health Leadership that it was developing. It involved working with three Schools of Public Health in California, Berkeley, Los Angeles, and San Diego, as well as developing and implementing a leadership training program for State and County level public health administrators. I accepted this assignment, but I knew that this was a transition period for me while I was contemplating my next professional journey. I was even asked to accept a full-time position at the Western Consortium as the Training Director, but I was not ready to make that commitment.

And then another person/mentor entered my life at this juncture, John O'Neal, President of the California School of Professional Psychologists. I was impressed by his recently published book, "The Paradox of Leadership", that also dealt with the Dark side of leadership and the leadership exhaustion factor. I consulted with him regarding my dilemma - how to make the shift from a structured and prestigious position to an unstructured life in a relatively unknown or unexplored professional environment. He suggested that either I start writing about my life or join an educational program. He recommended that I explore the California Institute of Integral Studies, founded by Haridass Chowdhury, a disciple of Aurovindo, in India.

I decided to explore that and registered in their new Integral Health Studies Program, to pursue a Diploma in Integral Health. That Program introduced me to other systems of Health, including Ayurvedic, Chinese, and Energetic healing. This was a mind-opening experience for me, as I began to explore how I could combine my conventional medicine knowledge with other systems of health care and shift my own consciousness from curing or symptomatic treatment to wholistic healing and wellness, especially for women. I completed this program and graduated in 1996, getting my Diploma in Integral Health. I was selected to lead my class in the Graduation ceremony held in San Francisco.

During this period, I also pursued a Home-Study program in Homeopathy from The Institute of Homeopathy, based in the United Kingdom, and received a Diploma in Homeopathy after completing this program.

While wondering how I would use this knowledge to help women in health and healing, a Vision came to me one day when I was dancing in my home in Fremont - Create a Center for Women's Health and Wellness and call it *The Healing Well*. By this time, we had also purchased a home in a beautiful community in the North Coast of the Sonoma County called The Sea Ranch. That seemed to be the perfect place to launch The Healing Well.

In 1998, I created The Healing Well, a Center in Gualala, a small town in the Mendocino County near The Sea Ranch. The Center would focus on promoting women's health in the community. My Vision was based on women's wisdom and trust in their own feelings, about their healing and wholeness. It was to be a place where women could share their unique knowledge about their health from personal stories and learn about possibilities, resources, and approaches to enhance their power to create ongoing health and wholeness in their lives. It called for integrating body, mind, and spiritual practices in their daily lives.

9

The Healing Well

My Vision of the Healing Well was based on women's freedom and trust in their own feelings about their own healing and wholeness. I visualized The Healing Well's concept on a well, a place of unique times and, even today in many parts of the world, a place where women come for water and tend to share information about their lives. My Center, The Healing Well, offered women's health circles on: Choices in Healing and Wholeness; Health, Movement, and Energy balance classes; Resources and creativity through writing and art, Integral Health Promoting lessons; dialogues and consultations on managing mid-life changes; and membership to its well-stocked library of books, audio/video tapes on women's health and related issues.

Many women from the California North Coast communities, The Sea Ranch, Gualala, Point Arena, and Mendocino, came to The Healing Well to seek information, participate in the dialogues/ workshops, and share their personal stories and experiences in their lives that influenced, supported, or destroyed their health and wellness.

The Healing Well was a sacred place, unique for women, by women, and about women, to talk freely and learn from their personal experiences and stories about their health and healing. I felt that I brought to The Healing Well, my entire life experience of working with and supporting women in their health and healing. It was a culmination of my lifetime's work in women's health.

Over the next five years, 1998-2003, more than a hundred women from our communities attended various classes, discussion groups, and healing circles. I offered an eight-week series in integrating Body/Mind/Spirit practices in daily life for health and healing, a four-week series on Pathways to Health; Sessions on Awakening the Healer Within through self-care practices; Creative practices to boost our healing; Writing for our Healing; Practices to reduce stress; Qigong Practices, etc.

In 2003, we constructed an extra room attached to our house in The Sea Ranch to provide the space I needed to continue my writing and healing circles. I then closed the office in Gualala and moved my activities to our home, where I continued to hold small circles for women in health and healing.

My focus also began to shift to my writing and on one-to-one or smaller circles, mainly for Spiritual practices in healing and awakening the Healer Within. I also began to volunteer for the local Hospice Services under the Redwood Coast Medical Services, where I was serving as a Board Member. Sometimes, the Hospice clients were referred to The Healing Well for healing and respite. As a physician, one learns to keep the patient alive at any cost, so I was inexperienced at assisting/helping someone to die peacefully. I was learning about the Dance of Life. Death and Rebirth, embracing it all with grace and presence. Working with the Hospice Volunteers was a major turning point in my professional life.

I began to feel a shift in my own consciousness and took some time off from many activities in which I was engaged.

And The Healing Well Continues Within Me

In 2005, I was reaching an important landmark in my life. I was entering my sixty-fifth year. Something was shifting in me.

Volunteering with the local Hospice reminded me of my own mortality. I was growing older. How would I remain active, engaged, and vital until the end of my life? Who would show me this path and teach me how to make this journey gracefully?

The Healing Well had been functioning for seven years and I was continuing to hold small circles of women on Healing and Wellness, in my home. My beloved husband Steve's health was declining. We needed to be closer to some health care services. We bought a second home in Santa Rosa and began to spend part of our time there, connecting with the relevant health care facilities. We also began to travel specially to meet our families and some close friends. I started writing about my life and especially about what The Healing Well meant to me.

My consciousness was shifting. I started exploring the topic of Aging and connecting with individuals and groups for discussions, sometimes just listening to their stories. I invited eight women who had attended my Healing Well sessions at the *Well* and who were also growing older. Most of them by then were 65 years and older. We formed a circle of six women, Ruth, Cynthia, Adele, Sussanah, Mary Rhyne, and me and started meeting at the Point Arena Senior Center, where Adele worked. We called ourselves, "A Circle of Vital Women". We shared our lives' journeys, the challenges, and how we were dealing with those. All of us wanted to stay vital and active till the end of our lives.

I also began to read books especially written by women who have been exploring the topics of aging and how this was affecting their lives. Noteworthy among these were:

Carolyn Heilburn's *book, "The Last Gift of Time: Life beyond 60"*. Carolyn writes about her desire for solitude, how she became conscious of the most precious gift we have *-time - e*specially at this phase of our lives.

Hen Co-op's book, *"Growing Old Disgracefully-New Ideas for Getting the Most Out of Life"* in which women share their life stories and talk about what they left behind as they were getting older, old identities, old patterns, and early role models.

Judith Duerk's book, *"Circle of Stones"*, once again encouraged me in this new direction and I realized that I must refocus The Healing Well. I wanted to connect with women of my age and even older and share our journeys, learn, and support each other. We renamed our Circle to "CLUB-400"; we had eight women and together had accumulated 400 years of life. The name gave us a joyful and positive outlook on our lives. Together we had a lot of experience to share.

This Circle met monthly for four years. We shared our life stories, some of which we had never shared with anyone before. The act of remembering our life stories was powerful and healing. We talked about the challenges of end-of-life care and death. Some of us were experiencing serious health challenges, either our own or our life-partner's. Some had to move out of the area to be either closer to some family members or to health care facilities (as Gualala had only a small health center). Two of our members passed away leaving big holes in our hearts. I too experienced that attending to these changing issues of life was important and some called for making changes in our lifestyles.

And The Third Journey Begins

On December 19, 2008, I celebrated my 69th birthday, an important landmark. I realized that I was now entering the seventh decade of my life, after this year. Age 70 is an important year of one's life. To reach this age is not uncommon these days, and to arrive at this decade of one's life in a relatively sound body, mind, and spiritual health, is a gift and a great blessing. The life expectancy in my family had not been long. My father died at age 59, my mother at 70, and my elder sister at age 69. I was very aware of that but also felt that it was a gift that I was at this age in fairly good health. From now on, it becomes not just a question of adding Years to Life, but rather adding Life to Years. I wanted to again connect with women closer to my age, who were interested in pursuing this phase of their lives' journey together.

I sent an invitation to some women in their sixties and beyond in my community to form a Circle. In January 2009, a group of ten women met at our home in The Sea Ranch. We decided to create a Circle and call it "Sisters of The Third Journey".

During the years 2009-2015, we met first every month, then every other month, and in the last two years once quarterly.

Transitions

One of the important challenges we all face during this phase of our lives are *Transitions,* many major ones that call for important shifts in how and where we might live. These can be major health issues either in us or affecting our life-partner; physical and financial issues that create limitations etc.

During this period, we *lost* one "sister"; two left the Circle due to personal reasons and three others moved away physically from the area, making it difficult for them to attend our meetings. But we also gained two new members. Several of us were in transitions, either in relationship with our partners, or in our place of living. My life-partner, the love of my life, Steve's health was declining and by 2012 we were spending more time in our home in Santa Rosa. Steve passed away in 2013. My dear friend Ruth had also lost her partner, Carlton, earlier and she returned to Santa Rosa from Boise Idaho, where she had gone a few years earlier with her husband to be closer to his family. I sold our house in The Sea Ranch, as I could not see myself living alone there, and moved full time to Santa Rosa. It took a couple of years to sort out all the paperwork and formalities after Steve's death. I had to start thinking about living alone at this phase of my life; what I call solo-aging.

By 2015, three members of The Third Journey Circle moved to Oakmont, an active senior community in Santa Rosa, in the Valley of the Moon area. Another person moved in 2016 and a new person joined our Circle. I also sold my house in Santa Rosa in 2016 and moved to Oakmont, where I had earlier bought a small house. These selling and moving from two large houses to one small house required getting rid of a lot of furniture and other personal items. I invited my family, nephew and niece, to take whatever they wanted and gave away the rest to friends and charities. This was a grieving experience, as I was letting go of a big part of my previous life. But one must, what I call, "lighten the load" as one moves on to older years and especially when one is solo-aging.

In 2016, with another new member joining the Circle, we decided to call it "Sisters of The Third Journey Phase II". We continued to meet once a month in our homes in Oakmont, where most of us now lived. By now, we were all moving into our seventh decade of life.

When we consciously pursue our lives from the fifth decade onwards, we notice changes that are occurring in our lives and the challenges that present themselves, sometimes unexpectedly. We learn to adjust, adapt, and often make changes that our lives demand of us - sometimes reluctantly, sometimes actively. No one is fully prepared for getting older and of course we all were getting older. We were noticing new needs, such as solitude, wanting to slow down, and most importantly the preciousness of time.

Some of the challenges and concerns that came up at our gatherings were:

1. What does Aging mean to me? Am I comfortable with growing older?

2. What changes can I expect in my physical body and mental state of my being over the next 10-20 years? What am I doing or can do to take care of myself? Am I nurturing myself? Am I gracefully accepting these changes and letting go of unreasonable expectations from myself?

3. What changes are occurring or might occur in my relationships, with my partner/my children/grandchildren/friends? How am I preparing for that?

4. Where is the best place for me to live now? What is more important: Access to services? Nature? Proximity to relatives who might be of help if needed? Closer to like-minded people? What are Pro and Cons for each of these?

5. Do I have enough financial resources to carry me through 'til the end of my life? How do I best manage what I have? If not, then what are the options?

6. How do I stay creative and mentally active? What will I do if I notice a decline in my state of mental well-being? What are the options? Am I prepared for that?

7. How do I keep joy and laughter and fun in my life?

8. How do I find Meaning in my life during the Third Journey? What really matters now? What do I let go of in what doesn't serve my life now? What remains to be done and why?

9. What does "Spirit" mean to me? What spiritual practices have meaning for me?

I felt that it was time for me to focus on **"What Really Matters?"**.

10

And The Journey Continues

One of the challenges we face when getting older, generally after 70, is how to remain actively engaged in life, especially if one's health is reasonably good. Fortunately, my health remains good with a few issues (diabetes, high blood pressure), but under good control. Even though I am a medical doctor, I tend to avoid doctors and medical procedures as much as I can. I don't have too much confidence in today's conventional medical practice. It tends to rely more on medical tests and procedures than on physician's personal assessment. Fortunately, I have found a good Integral Medical Practitioner as my physician, who is not aggressive regarding laboratory tests and procedures. I also consult with an Ayurvedic practitioner, I too have a good knowledge about Ayurveda, for supplemental treatments.

In 2013, I was invited by the Sonoma County Area Agency for Aging to become a member of its Advisory Council. This was a great opportunity to learn about and connect with the services and challenges for seniors living in Sonoma County. I learnt that a significant population of the Sonoma County is low-income. The County also has significantly high proportion of seniors, i.e., age 60 and over. Among the challenges this population faces are affordable housing, nourishing food availability, and social isolation. Many older people live alone, and many are isolated, too poor to afford the collective housing accommodation. There are also several beautiful senior residential communities, but not affordable for everyone. Personally, I do not like senior residential communities, especially where you share meals and all other recreational activities with others, who have occasional visits from younger members of their families. I have visited many of these and always come back feeling depressed. Steve and I had looked at some when we were thinking of getting a place in Santa Rosa. Steve's comment was that there were too many old people there. Of course, these were senior communities. (In fact, now I live in an active senior community, but these are independent homes with interesting services offered for fun and recreation and connecting with others. Here, it is up to each person or couple to join or not. Even though it is a safe and comfortable community, I do not feel energized here. There is too much "old white people energy" that does not stimulate me. I am used to living in a diverse community and am still open-minded about finding that in Northern California.)

I also became interested in Palliative Care/End of Life Care. I took a course with the Jewish Family and Children's Support Services and became a trained facilitator in Palliative/End-of-Life Care. I worked with one-on-one clients. I found this very challenging as I had to learn to be a very patient listener and observe and respond as the person shared or showed some needs. There are no set recipes for this phase of one's life journey. I found that this was not something I wanted to continue doing, as it was a bit depressing.

In 2014, I visited India and learnt about and visited a Program in Vrindavan for abandoned widows. Maitri-India, a non-profit organization headed by Winnie and Bhopinder Singh, had started building a Home for the Widows. I also learnt about some other Agencies providing shelter and education for abandoned children in two orphanages. I was very moved to do something substantial for girls and older abandoned women in India. I felt this was my way of paying back to my Mother Country, that had given me so much.

In 2015, I created a Foundation, Saraswati Foundation, with the aim to empower girls and women from low-income communities, through education and income-generation opportunities. I selected four projects initially:

1. Widows of Vrindavan: Provide shelter and Income-Generation opportunities.
2. Sri Rama Ashram in Haridwar: Provide scholarships for girls pursuing health-related career.
3. Anantha Ashram Orphanage in Hisoor, near Bangalore: Provide education for children.
4. An Odissi Dance School for girls from very low-income families in Bhubaneswar, Odissa. This school was started by Guru Jyoti Rout, who is the Founder and Teacher of in Kala Mandir College of Odissi Dance in Fremont.

I set up this Foundation to be managed by The Tides Foundation, in San Francisco. This also gave me an opportunity to visit India every year, if possible, to see and connect with these projects.

By 2017, I felt that I was fully engaged in my life beyond 70 with the Sonoma County Area Agency for Aging Advisory Council, Palliative-End of Life Care with JFCS, Conscious Aging Circles, Third Journey Circle, and Saraswati Foundation. In 2017, I also joined the Valley of the Moon Rotary Club in Oakmont.

By the end of 2017, especially, after the experience with two big fires that threatened my home, I felt a big shift in my consciousness. I felt the vulnerability of life and the need for some changes in the pursuit of my life in its few remaining and precious years.

And The Fourth Journey Begins – 2018

In 2018, I entered the last year of my seventies; soon, in 2019, I would turn 80. Wow! I never really thought that I would live this long. I began to become more acutely conscious of my remaining time on this Planet Earth.

I began to ask again: *"What Really Matters Now"?* What is unfinished? What do I want to do now that would have meaning in my life? What is important to maintain the quality of my life? Who do I connect with? And more questions about life at this juncture. It may be short, a few months/even days! Or longer, a few years maybe! I didn't know, but I did know that I want to get the most out of whatever time remains. There were no clear answers here. I knew that I had to clear my time, open myself to experience every day fully, be aware, and attend to my own needs.

In 2016, I had moved to this "Active Adult Community" (a euphemism) in Oakmont. And I had Joy, my little dachshund dog, who came from Fairbanks, Alaska with Sandy, four months old then, and now an important being in my life. (Sometimes I think she is the Spirit of Steve, reincarnated).

I felt the need to free myself from my many commitments, to free my time. I resigned from the Sonoma County Area Agency for Aging and from the Jewish Family and Children's Support Services. For a year, I also took a break from the Third Journey Group. My only regular commitment was the VOM Rotary Club, though at times I wondered whether I should have joined it. But I felt at that time that it would be a good way to connect with other members of this community, as well as some of the local community service Organizations that the Club supported. In 2021, I decided to leave the Rotary Club also to free up from any set commitments.

So, the question that I ask: How do I visualize this part of my life's journey?

What really matters to me Now?

I feel that this phase of life should be to stay connected or reenforce connection to myself, my *Inner Being.* This should be a journey of *Being* rather than *Doing.* This is not something I have been good at. I am much better with *Doing.* Just *Being,* I feel, is a waste of time. I always feel that I should be doing something, achieving something tangible, that I feel proud of or satisfied with, that I have made myself useful to the world.

I must learn to be *"old"* or find inspiration from writing/ experiences of others who have made this journey. Learn how to feel comfortable with my life as it unfolds and how to be still at times and just listen to my breath-my body-my spirit.

An Interesting and inspiring thought from a poem:

"Fearless Out of the Wisdom", from the Sage's Tao Te Ching Ancient Advice for the Second Half of Life:

> *"Discovering my strengths has been a benefit.*
> *But discovering my true weaknesses and*
> *Acknowledging them to myself*
> *I see myself for who I am.*
> *No illusions*
> *Great Serenity."*

Another relevant passage from "Autumn Conscious Eldering and Aging Consciously", by Ron Pevny, resonated with me.:

"In these dark months of the year, our psyches call us to direct our energies toward our inner lives, as we seek the guidance for the journey forward that can come only from befriending our inner-

voice- the voice that knows our unique path toward the wholeness of conscious elderhood – the voice that is our only realistic map through the mysterious and dangerous territory. That lies within and without."

In my Fourth Journey, I feel that I need to savor life, focusing more on being and less on doing. Learning how to balance doing and being is a critical challenge for me.

"Can I change my perception of my life now?" I ask.

The answer comes:

"OLD MAPS NO LONGER WORK"

At this phase of my life, I keep wanting to have a clear Map that would give me direction, challenge, and clear pathways, or even some not so clear. But I am realizing that "Old Maps" no longer work, because I keep looking at the paths I have taken before, the directions I have followed, and the challenges that came my way, some that I was able to cope with, some remained unresolved. I try to look at my old map of life; maybe there is some hidden road, may be something that I missed or remained unresolved, that I can pursue now.

But no, as Joyce Rupp writes in her poem:

> *"There is nothing there now,*
> *   Except some well-travelled paths,*
> *They have seen my footsteps often-*
> *   Held my laughter, caught my tears.*
> *I keep going over the old map-*
> *   But now the roads lead nowhere.*
> *It seems that there is a meaningless wilderness*
> *   Where life is dull and futile.*

"Toss away the old map", she says,
    It's no use where you're going.
But I must have a map, I say
    I can't be without direction.
She says, "So, why not let go, be free?"
    'Whatever, will I do? '- wails my security.
"Trust me", says my old/experienced soul.
    "But how will I know where to go?
    How will I find my way with no map?"
But then my soul cries out-
    'Just be a pilgrim- travel by the Stars'.

So, I feel, it's time for the pilgrim in me to travel in the dark, to learn to read the stars that shine in my soul. I will walk deeper into the dark of my night. I will trust the guidance of the stars and let their light be enough for me.

This is the time for closing some accounts.

My Life is coming to a full circle.

And The Circle Continues

Some meaningful statements, from others and me) that have inspired me and helped me in my moving forward in life, especially at the later phase of my Third Journey and the beginning of the Fourth:

"Living Well - means, living a life of meaning. Be certain that you do not die without having done something wonderful for humanity."

"I have moved and lived in so many places in the world that Geography, as such, has no meaning for me. Culture - Yes."

"I am convinced that most people do not grow up. We mostly grow old."

"We carry cumulative years in our bodies."

"Inside us is the *home* – the only place where we belong."

"Faith is the evidence of things not seen".

"In three words, I can sum up everything I learnt about life. *It goes on.*"

Some of the Questions/Ideas that I am pursuing now, as I move into the Fourth Journey of my Life:

1. I want to feel free to use my time as I want to.
2. I want to be conscious about maintaining my health and well-being.
3. I want to play more: With Joy, see movies/plays, listen to good music/dance/do some art?
4. I want to listen to my heart and my mind and do what they ask of me - rest if it wants/ read/ or do nothing- Perhaps the hardest part for me.
5. I want to write:
   a. Journal of The Third Journey: Challenges and Op portunities that we confronted and explored.
   b. My personal Memoir: *Dancing Feet In a Man's World*.
   c. My reflections on Aging, its many perspectives, may be as a series of articles for publication.
   d. Something about my work on Leadership.
6. How do I connect with the younger generation of my family? Or even other more like-minded people? Sometimes I wonder if moving to a mostly white/senior community at this phase of my life was a good idea. At times I feel isolated. May be this is another transitional

home. I do want to explore other options while I still am in good health and energy.

Most importantly, I must remain open to:

The Unexpected
    New Options
        Acceptance of Change that may come

AND MY STORY CONTINUES - 2023 AND BEYOND

I AM NOT DONE YET WITH LIFE.

Final Thought

Reflections On A Life Well Lived

This is the story of my Life's journey. I do believe that it has been a unique journey and sharing it with other women, especially the younger ones, will help validate their experiences. Even though the world is changing, and women are in a different place in many societies than they were 50 years ago, for many, not much has changed. In some places it might have gone backward. I hope that my story offers glimpses of hope and courage to others wanting to break through traditional values which are still imposed upon women (more than on men). And when these women reach a critical mass, a shift will occur. It will no longer be a Man's World, rather One World with equal rights and opportunities for both women and men.

Most of us hope that when we leave the Planet Earth, we will leave something of ourselves behind by which, with a bit of luck, others will remember and honor us. For some it might be a book, for some a building with their names on it, for some a successful business. For others it might be children or passing on a family name. However, this dream does not always come true.

I do not have an ambition to leave monuments by which people would remember me. I also did not have children of my own to pass on my family name. But now, in the dwindling years of my life, I feel that I do harbor some wish - to leave a record of my life's journey of some of the challenges I faced as a Woman in a Man's World; to tell the story of the opportunities I had and the paths I chose, the countries where I served, in fact where I spent Love, hoping to have helped others to take leadership in serving their communities and to have empowered local community leaders, especially women.

Although, there may not be many outward signs remaining of what I believed was my contribution, I know that I will always love the countries and their people and will always treasure the memories of the years I was privileged to serve, even though I realize that there will never be a monument in my name.

I feel that I am like a farmer who knows that no matter how well she plows, seeds, and fertilizes and no matter how much fruit her efforts bear, in autumn, the fruit of her labor will be cut to the ground. No matter how excellent and useful they might have been, they no longer stand. I guess, most of us realize this later in our lives and need to know that our lifework mattered, that our efforts made a difference, and that we are worthy of respect.

When all is said and done, I feel that I will be known not for how hard I worked or what I achieved, but for how well I loved what I did, how well I lived my life, and hopefully, how well I opened many doors for women who came later.

AND THE JOURNEY CONTINUES 'TIL THE FINAL BREATH IS TAKEN.

Sumedha Mona Khanna

Acknowledgement

My life story will not be complete without mentioning the people who had important influence on my character, my thinking, and my work. Most of them were women, and yes, there were a few men who inspired me and had faith in me, who helped move me further in my professional career because of their trust in my strength and capability. I believe that we don't do anything alone; we are in relation to something or someone. It is important to recognize and honor those who have been an important part of our life's journey. I call them Fellow Travelers, Mentors, or Inspirational Leaders.

My Parents

I am deeply indebted to my parents, Din Diyal and Krishna Kumari Khanna, who brought me into this world. My father was a loving and gentle person, deeply committed to his family and his work in education. Throughout his life he engaged in the field of education. His humility, dedication to his students, special concern about the advancement of women, punctuality and management of time, honesty, incorruptibility, even though all his life he worked under bureaucracy), and his sense of humor and love of music, are some of the qualities I admired and perhaps inherited. My mother was a strong woman, a Vedic scholar who had great knowledge of the Vedas, the Hindu culture, and religious scriptures. She was an ardent worshipper of the Divine Feminine, something that we all inherited. She strongly believed in the education of girls, even during the period when girls' education was not considered a priority. Her sophistication: less or cheap was not accepted and her strong and independent nature had great influence on us girls. Both my parents encouraged our education and did not force the traditional cultural values.

My School Teachers

Two teachers stand out who had influenced me in my early life. Khillo Devi, my math teacher, a Gandhian woman, tall and beautiful, always wore Khadi (home-spun cotton) sarees, who never married, and was a brilliant, straight-talk person who didn't waste words. I remember her keeping a word-fast one weekend in a month when she did not speak to anyone. This practice I also followed during a very busy period of my senior professional life, when I was also living alone. I felt that this practice helped me to recover my strength and concentration. I believe it was the influence of Khillo Devi that I just fell in love with math. I would read our school math book like a story book, - solving puzzles and remembering all the answers by heart.

Ms. Ratna, my chemistry teacher, was a diminutive, sharp-tongued woman from South India. She was a brilliant chemistry teacher and I believe recognized my scholastic tendency. She always encouraged me. I began to love chemistry and always excelled in that subject, securing 100% in the finals of the High School examination.

My professors in the Lady Hardinge Medical College

During my five years of medical studies, five professors stand out whom I admired, who inspired me, recognized my talent and scholastic achievement, and encouraged me to be the best. These were five very different natured women; each one was excellent in her field and deeply interested in their students. All were strong women, only one of them married.

Dr. Achaya, my Professor of Anatomy, was a strong and stern woman, very beautiful and of a grand stature. She projected strength and discipline and was always elegantly dressed. Everyone in the college feared her. Anatomy became my favorite subject. I loved the body form and structure and how the wonder of its various parts synchronized as a whole. In anatomy dissection, one must be precise. It requires total focus and I believe she introduced me to discipline, precision, total attention, and discipline. She was a great mentor in my early years of medical education.

Dr. Chowdhury, my Professor of Surgery, was a short, sharp-tongued woman, very focused, disciplined, and time conscious. She expected loyalty and discipline from her students. She was an excellent surgeon, a rarity for women those days. She also never married. Even though I was not her favorite student, I admired her strength, precision in diagnosis, and her surgical skills – some of the qualities I believe I have continued to inculcate in my professional and personal life.

Dr. Parvati Malkani, my Professor of Obstetrics and Gynecology, was a quiet, unassuming, short-statured, and very beautiful woman. I liked her gentle approach toward her patients and her full undivided attention to each one of them. She was a superb and patient teacher, very clear and encouraging. She also never married and lived with her family. I believe she had some influence in my choosing Obstetrics and Gynecology as my specialty. I also inherited her gentle quality of dealing with her patients, her thoroughness with the clinical examination and potential diagnosis through thorough, complete, physical, and medical examination. I was one of her favorite students and she encouraged me to pursue Ob/Gyn specialty.

Dr. Padmavati, My Professor of Internal Medicine, was a woman of medium stature with a strong presence, who commanded respect from all her junior residents and students. Even though Internal Medicine was not my favorite subject, Dr. Padmavati made it more interesting. In her teaching, she emphasized the importance of detailed medical history and a thorough clinical examination before ordering any laboratory tests etc. That was her strength and required sincere and attentive listening to the patient's story, as sometimes the details hidden in the patient's story gave a clue to not only the possible medical condition, but also the contributing factors to that condition. Unfortunately, this skill is now rare among the medical practitioners. There is too much reliance on diagnostic technology. I recall Dr. Padmavati's Grand Rounds in the medical wards, accompanied by her senior and junior residents and students. I believe the most important lessons I learnt from her were non-judgmental listening, giving the patient credit for her story, and patience in expecting a cure. (This was not easy for me, as I found the Internal Medicine too slow and so I didn't choose this as my specialty.)

Dr. Sumedha Pathak, my namesake - in fact, I was named after her by my mother. She was the daughter of a close friend of my mother. When I was born, she was just starting her medical education. My mother decided to give me the name Sumedha, hoping that I too would pursue a medical career, a wish that came true. I met Dr. Sumedha Pathak when I was in the third year of medical school. She was Associate Professor of Medicine. I clearly recall when I met her for the first time in class. I was sitting in the front row when she called me by my name, Sumedha. She had a sweet knowing smile. She was a tall, beautiful, and elegant woman, married to a surgeon. She was one of the most approachable professors in our college, very loving and non-threatening, a special quality appreciated by most students.

My Supervisors and Mentors in England

Two women, both Obstetricians and Gynecologists in the Elizabeth Garrett Anderson Hospital for women in London where I was a junior resident, became my early mentors as I embarked on my specialization in Obstetrics and Gynecology. I was fortunate to have had the opportunity of working with Ms. Mocata and Ms. Josephine Barnes. (In England, once a doctor specializes in a field and completes all requirements to become a specialist, she/he is addressed as Ms. or Mr. instead of doctor.) I believe working under their supervision at the beginning of my professional career in England was very fortuitous. I therefore consider them as my mentors.

Ms. Mocata was an elderly, tall, and slim person, with a gentle demeanor yet commanded a strong personality. She was very detailed and precise in her diagnostic and surgical procedure. Her clarity and depth, as well as care for her patients, were important qualities that had long-lasting impact on my own professional practice. At the end of my assignment, she gave me a detailed testimonial that was very helpful in my professional advancement.

Ms. Josephine Barnes was my second supervisor. Her personality was quite different from that of Ms. Mocata. She was gregarious and very observant of my technical skills and allowed me to do more surgeries under her supervision. She was well respected by The Royal College of OB/Gyn, and her testimonials and recommendations helped me in seeking higher level posts in London hospitals, as well as in my acceptance at the School of Public Health in the University of Pittsburgh, USA.

Wise Women in California, USA

After taking my early retirement from WHO, I moved to California where I began to seek a new vision for my professional work in health and healing. This was a period of change, both in myself as wanting to reconnect with my feminine self after working for more than 25 years of my life in a Man's World, as well as finding a new approach to promoting health and the healing of women. I had to move from being an active Ob/Gyn Practitioner to a facilitator and educator in integral health. This was not easy, and I actively sought the wisdom and ideas from women who were engaged in health and healing through their work and/or writing. I attended many workshops and read their writings. I met some of them and had the opportunity of consulting with them, seeking their advice. Through studying their lives and "listening" to their wisdom, I learned about their journeys, struggles, ideas, thoughts, and power. In a way, I created a collage of wisdom of many women: writers, artists, politicians, physicians, healers, and feminists.

While it is not possible to list each one of these women or write about their work and wisdom, I know that without their guidance, I wouldn't have been able to make this transition. The following are just some of these women who became my guides and teachers during this transition from medical to healing work.

Maya Angelou, Joan Anderson, Angeles Arrien, Jean Shinoda Bolen, Joan Borycenko, Joan Chittister, Judith Duerk, Carolyn Heilbrun, Deena Metzger, Maureen Murdoch, Christiane Northrup, and Tina Stromstead.

Through the work and wisdom of these women, I was able to create my own circle of wise women to guide me to find my own feminine power and wisdom that had been latent during the past 25 years of my work in a Man's World. As Maureen Murdock notes in her book, The Heroine's Journey ", for a woman to internalize the skills learned on a Hero's journey and integrate them with the wisdom of her heroine's journey, she has to undergo a "sacred marriage", a marriage of ego and self. The wisdom of these women guided me through my midlife journey into wholeness. I then wanted to be a guide to other women by sharing this newly acquired wisdom. This led to the creation of The Healing Well.

Even now, as I move into what I call my Fourth Journey, I search for and find women whose wisdom continues to guide me through this phase, especially as a solo ager having lost my life partner. My friends Ruth Hynds and Judith Duerk have been showing me how to move through this phase gracefully. And I discovered Joan Anderson, Joan Chittister, and Carolyn Heilbrun again. "The Gift of Years – Growing Old Gracefully" by Joan Chittister and "The Last Gift of Time" by Carolyn Heilbrun gave me new insight on how to move forward in my Fourth Journey of life - 80 and beyond with joy and grace. All we have to do at this phase of life is to live to the fullest and, if possible, a balanced life with some taking and some giving.

As one poet has said:

"When you come into this world,
        Bring something.
When you leave this world,
        Give something back."

I am very grateful for the guidance that I have received from the wise women and the support from some wise men (Samuel Wishik, Abraham Horwitz and my father Din Diyal Khanna) who believed in my potential and helped me to go forward in life. And I have been blessed with having a life partner who was also my soul-friend, with whom I spent 12 years of deep friendship prior to our marriage that lasted 27 + years, until he passed away. I am deeply grateful for his unlimited and unselfish love for me, and his belief in a positive approach to life, as expressed through his unforgettable words:

"Nothing is lost in God's Kingdom."

(Whenever I thought I couldn't find what I was looking for); and

"Everything works together in a sense of harmony, even when we don't recognize that."

Concluding Comment

I have written about my life's journey based on my memory or shall I say, "to the best of my recollection." I guess we are often left with a partial memory. As Maureen Murdock says, "What we remember is a reconstruction of image and feeling that suits our needs and purpose. Memory is a reflection of how we see ourselves. The way we tell our life story is the way we begin to live our life." We know that we usually remember images that carry strong feelings.

Basically, the qualities that have attracted me and sustained me in my life are:

Courage
    Purposefulness
        Commitment
            Visionary
                Tenacity
                    Analytical
                        Fearlessness
                          Humility
                              Leadership through example

✶ ✶ ✶ ✶ ✶ ✶

Sumedha Mona Khanna

Endnotes

1. Page iii: Genesis I.27. The full sentence is "So God created man in His own image, in the image of God created He him; male and female created He them". This quote is significant because of the powerful influence of Adhangini throughout Sumedha's life. A performance by Ravi Shankar's (World Renowned Sitar Player) brother (Uday Shankar), who was an exceptional dancer, in London in the 60's imprinted the significance of the understanding of women and men being each half of one unity, Human. In Hindu religion, the combined image of Shiva and his wife Parvati (who is also called Shakti), is called Ardhangini (half male/half female) incorporates man and woman in one image. This image symbolizes that together the male and female constitute on entity, a unity of Shiva and Shakti, Yin and Yang. This is a beautiful concept of unity and equality. But it remains only a beautiful aspiration. In real life such equality rarely exists. Yet, it has been my belief throughout my life. The image of Ardhangini, Shiva and Shakti, adorns my home temple and work area and continues to inspire me.

2. Page 21: The Elizabeth Garrett Anderson Hospital for Women was formed in Bloomsbury, London, in the United Kingdom by the amalgamation of the Obstetrics Hospital and the Elizabeth Garrett Anderson Hospital, in 2001. The new Hospital for Women developed from St. Mary's Dispensary in the 1870s. It was founded to enable poor women to obtain medical help from qualified female practitioners. In that era, this was a very unusual thing. In 1866, Elizabeth Garrett Anderson was appointed General Medical Attendant to St. Mary's Dispensary, where she worked for over 20 years, through the change to a new name. The foundation stone of the new building was laid by the Princess of Wales in 1889 and was named the Elizabeth Garrett Anderson Hospital in 1918.

3. Page 23: Queen Mary's Hospital for East End (1861-1983) was a historic hospital in the East End of London that started as a dispensary in 1861 by a local doctor- William Elliott. It was in an old house constructed from ship's timbers. In 1879 with additional funds donated a two-story new Dispensary with the motto "Ohne Zaagern und ohne Zagen" – (Without hesitation or Fear, translated from German)- was opened in 1879. It was converted into a hospital with 32 beds and was officially opened by the Duke of Westminster in 1890. It was further expanded through more donations and the hospital was renamed West Ham Hospital with 60 beds. In 1902 its name was changed again to West Ham and East London General Hospital. The hospital was then equipped with X-ray apparatus, electric lighting, and other needed equipment.

In 1909, further expansion was added, and the hospital was renamed the West Ham and Eastern General Hospital. Further expansion with addition of two new wards and other facilities took place in 1912-1913. During World War I, the Hospital offered 50 beds for Army use, thus became affiliated with the Royal Herbert Hospital in Woolwich. The Hospital continued to receive additional funds and acquired more land for its expansion. In 1916 King George V and Queen Mary visited the Hospital. With Queen Mary becoming its Patron in 1916, the Hospital was granted a Royal Charter in 1917 and changed its name to Queen Mary's Hospital for the East End.

After WWI, the Hospital received more donations and was frequently visited by several members of the Royal Family. In 1923, the Hospital added a Maternity Wing and a nurses' Home. It then had 160 beds. With the establishment of a new out-patient department, which would also be the War Memorial of the County Borough of West Ham, formally opened by Prince Henry at 11.00 am on 11th November 1924, this was the largest war memorial of any kind in Great Britain.

Further expansion of the Hospital continued and by 1938, the hospital had 219 beds with several specialized units. During WWII the hospital was evacuated and became a Casualty Hospital for air-raid casualties and sick and wounded servicemen. It was the first London hospital to be bombed in 1940. Even after subsequent repairs, the number of beds reduced to 164 and in 1979 it had only 106 beds.

Queen Mary's Hospital, the oldest voluntary hospital in West Ham, London was finally closed in 1983, when Newsham General Hospital opened. By 2003, most of the hospital buildings were demolished apart from the preserved Entry Archway with the Inscription- "Queen Mary's Hospital for East End"- that can just be discerned.

(Ref: Parsons J 1962, a Short History of Queen Mary's Hospital for The East End, London.)

4. Page 25: (Lost Hospitals of London: 1890 – current)
    Another historic hospital in the County of Surrey, south of London opened in 1839 as Epsom Union Workhouse. In 1840 infirm inmates of the Old Poor House were transferred to a ward in the main building. In 1851, a detached Infirmary was erected and in 1882 another Infirmary with 120 beds was built to the east of Workhouse. Further additions took place between 1888-1910- by 1922, the Infirmary had 153 beds. More buildings and facilities were added including a Nurses' Home, a Maternity Ward with 60 beds and an Emergency Medical Service.

    In 1948, the Hospital joined the National Health service under the control of the Epsom Group Hospital Management Committee and was renamed EPSOM DISTRICT HOSPITAL. By this time, it had 360 general beds, and the Workhouse buildings on the west of the site became the OAKS (Home for the Aged). Other additions in the 1950's modernized the hospital. It was finally opened in 1955 by Princess Margaret. By 1959, the hospital had 311 beds.

In 1974, following a major reorganization of the National Health Service, the hospital came under the administration of the Mid-Surrey District Health Authority as part of the South-West Thames Regional Health Authority. The hospital now had 405 acute beds and 82 psychiatric beds.

In 1990, with NHS reorganization once again, the hospital came under the control of The Epsom Healthcare Trust. In 1999, the Trust merged with the St. Hellier NHS Trust to form the Epsom and St. Hellier Hospital NHS Trust. The hospital continues to change with reorganization of NHS and though it is still in operation, its future is uncertain.

References

1. The Heroine's Journey: A woman's quest for Wholeness: Maureen Murdock; Shambala Publications, Inc. 1990
2. A Walk on The Beach: Tales of Wisdom from An Unconventional Woman; Joan Anderson; Broadway Books, 2004
3. The Road Back to Yourself: The Second Journey; Joan Anderson, Hyperion Books, 2008
4. Writing a Woman's Life; Carolyn G. Heilbrun; Ballantine Books, New York, 1988
5. The Last Gift of Time: Life Beyond Sixty; Carolyn Heilbrun; Ballantine Books, New York, 1997
6. Crossing To Avalon: A Woman's Midlife Pilgrimage; Jean Shinoda Bolen, M.D.; Harper, San Francisco 1994
7. The Gift of Years: Growing Old Gracefully; Joan Chittister, BlueBridge, 2008
8. The Heart of a Woman; Maya Angelou; Bantam Books, 1981
9. The Circle of Stones, Woman's Journey to Herself; Judith Duerk, Innisfree Press, 1993
10. A God Who Looks Like Me, Discovering A Woman-Affirming Spirituality; Patricia Lynn Reilly, Ballantine Books, New York, 1995
11. A Woman's Book of Life; Joan Borysenko, PhD., Riverhead Books, New York, 1996
12. Growing Old Disgracefully; New Ideas for Getting the Most Out of Life; The Hen Co-op; The Crossing Press, Freedom, CA, 1994
13. The Healing Well, My Midlife Journey into Wholeness; Sumedha Mona Khanna, M.D.; Birth A Book; 2011
14. Unreliable Truth: On Memoir and Memory; Maureen Murdock, SEAL PRESS 2003

✶ ✶ ✶ ✶ ✶ ✶